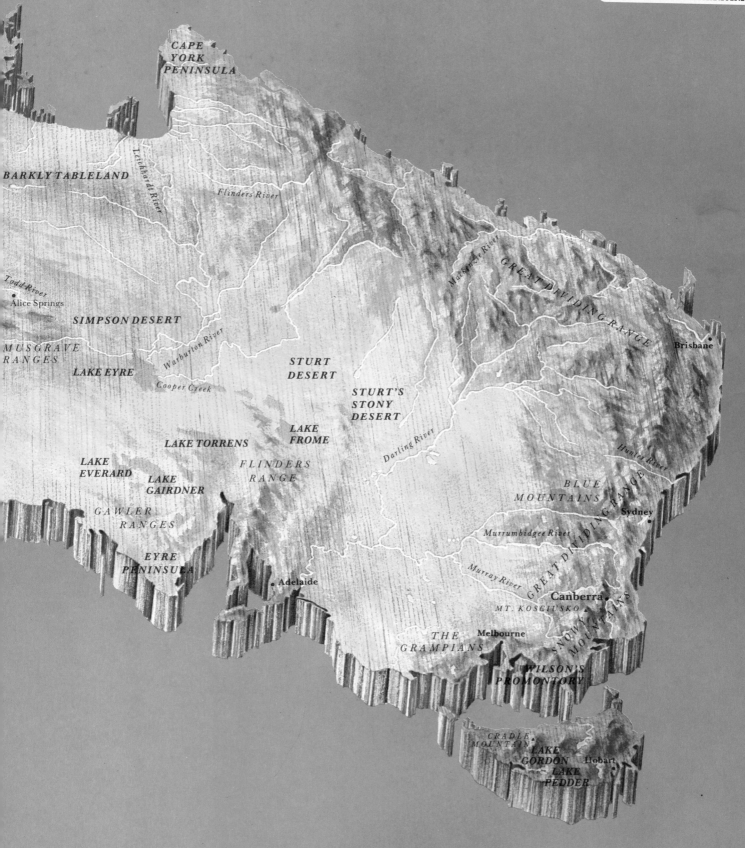

CAPE
YORK
PENINSULA

BARKLY TABLELAND

Leichhardt River

Flinders River

Todd River
• Alice Springs

SIMPSON DESERT

Mackenzie River

GREAT DIVIDING RANGE

MUSGRAVE
RANGES

Warburton River

STURT
DESERT

• Brisbane

LAKE EYRE

Cooper Creek

STURT'S
STONY
DESERT

LAKE TORRENS

LAKE
FROME

Darling River

LAKE
EVERARD

FLINDERS
RANGE

Hunter River

LAKE
GAIRDNER

BLUE
MOUNTAINS

GAWLER
RANGES

• Sydney

GREAT DIVIDING RANGE

Murrumbidgee River

EYRE
PENINSULA

Murray River

• Adelaide

Canberra •

MT. KOSCIUSKO •

SNOWY MOUNTAINS

THE
GRAMPIANS

Melbourne •

WILSON'S
PROMONTORY

CRADLE
MOUNTAIN

LAKE
GORDON

Hobart •

LAKE
PEDDER

AUSTRALIA

AUSTRALIA

By the Editors of Time-Life Books

TIME-LIFE BOOKS · AMSTERDAM

A CHILD'S FIRST LIBRARY OF LEARNING
VOYAGE THROUGH THE UNIVERSE
MYSTERIES OF THE UNKNOWN
TIME-LIFE HISTORY OF THE WORLD
FITNESS, HEALTH & NUTRITION
HEALTHY HOME COOKING
UNDERSTANDING COMPUTERS
THE ENCHANTED WORLD
LIBRARY OF NATIONS
HOME REPAIR AND IMPROVEMENT
CLASSICS OF EXPLORATION
PLANET EARTH
PEOPLES OF THE WILD
THE EPIC OF FLIGHT
THE SEAFARERS
WORLD WAR II
THE GOOD COOK
THE TIME-LIFE ENCYCLOPAEDIA
OF GARDENING
THE GREAT CITIES
THE OLD WEST
THE WORLD'S WILD PLACES
LIFE LIBRARY OF PHOTOGRAPHY
TIME-LIFE LIBRARY OF ART
GREAT AGES OF MAN
LIFE SCIENCE LIBRARY
LIFE NATURE LIBRARY

TIME-LIFE BOOKS

EDITOR-IN-CHIEF (Europe): Sue Joiner
European Executive Editor: Gillian Moore
Design Director: Ed Skyner
Assistant Design Director: Mary Staples
Chief of Research: Vanessa Kramer
Chief Sub-Editor: Ilse Gray

LIBRARY OF NATIONS

Editorial Staff for *Australia*
Editor: Tony Allan
Researcher: Krystyna Mayer
Designer: Lynne Brown
Sub-Editor: Sally Rowland
Picture Department: Christine Hinze, Peggy Tout
Editorial Assistant: Molly Oates

EDITORIAL PRODUCTION

Chief: Jane Hawker
Traffic Co-ordinators: Alan Godwin, Maureen Kelly
Editorial Department: Theresa John, Debra Lelliott,
Sylvia Osborne

Valuable help was given in the preparation of this
volume by John Dunn (Melbourne).

CONSULTANTS: Professor Geoffrey C. Bolton,
Head of the Australian Studies Centre at the
University of London, is the author of many
books and articles about Australian history. He is
the editor of the forthcoming five-volume *Oxford
History of Australia*. Craig McGregor is one of
Australia's leading social commentators and
journalists. His books include *Profile of Australia*
and *The Australian People*.

Contributors: The chapter texts were written by:
Philip Beard, Windsor Chorlton, Alan Lothian
and Craig McGregor.

Cover: An ancient desert oak stands alone in the
flat landscape bordering a highway in the
Northern Territory. In the background are the
violet domes of the Olgas, ancient mountains
worn smooth by erosion.

Pages 1 and 2: On page 1 is the emblem of
Australia, consisting of a shield bearing the
badges of the six states enclosed within an ermine
border signifying federation. The crest is a seven-
pointed star, six points of which represent the
states and the seventh the nation's two federal
territories. The shield is supported by a kangaroo
and an emu, and the whole emblem is adorned
with the wattle plant. The national flag is shown
on page 2.

Front and back endpapers: A topographic map
showing the major rivers, plains, mountain
ranges and other natural features of Australia
appears on the front endpaper; the back endpaper
shows the country's states and territories, as well
as the major towns.

This volume is one in a series of books describing
countries of the world—their natural resources, peoples,
histories, economies and governments.

XXXXXXXXXX

CONTENTS

In Sydney, Australia's oldest and largest city, the gleaming skyscrapers of the business district tower above wharfside buildings of an earlier era. In the

two centuries since British settlers first landed at nearby Sydney Cove, Australia has become a largely urban nation.

A LAND OF CLIMATIC EXTREMES

Over much of Australia, the climate is hot and dry. The continent lies at the world's most arid latitude, where sub-tropical high-pressure systems reliably produce day after day of clear skies. Rainfall is generally slight and the evaporation rate high. Surface water throughout the interior is scarce, and a huge band of desert sweeps across the centre of the continent.

Great variations occur, however. The tropical north is influenced by the North–East Asia Monsoon, and summer rains are heavy. The eastern coast is relatively well watered by the prevailing south-easterly trade winds, which shed much of their moisture over the Eastern Highlands. In winter, westerly winds bring high rainfall to the south-west coast and to Tasmania.

- TROPICAL
- SUB-TROPICAL
- TEMPERATE
- SEMI-DESERT
- DESERT

WESTERN AUSTRALIA
NORTHERN TERRITORY
QUEENSLAND
SOUTH AUSTRALIA
NEW SOUTH WALES
VICTORIA
TASMANIA

In a remote region of the Northern Territory, a tourist bus negotiates a dirt track through a rugged outback landscape. Since the 1970s Australia's

hinterland—little developed because of its low rainfall—has attracted a growing number of visitors, drawn by its austere beauty.

Refreshed by a morning swim, three Aboriginal youngsters relax near a Darwin beach. Thousands of Aboriginals died off under the initial impact of

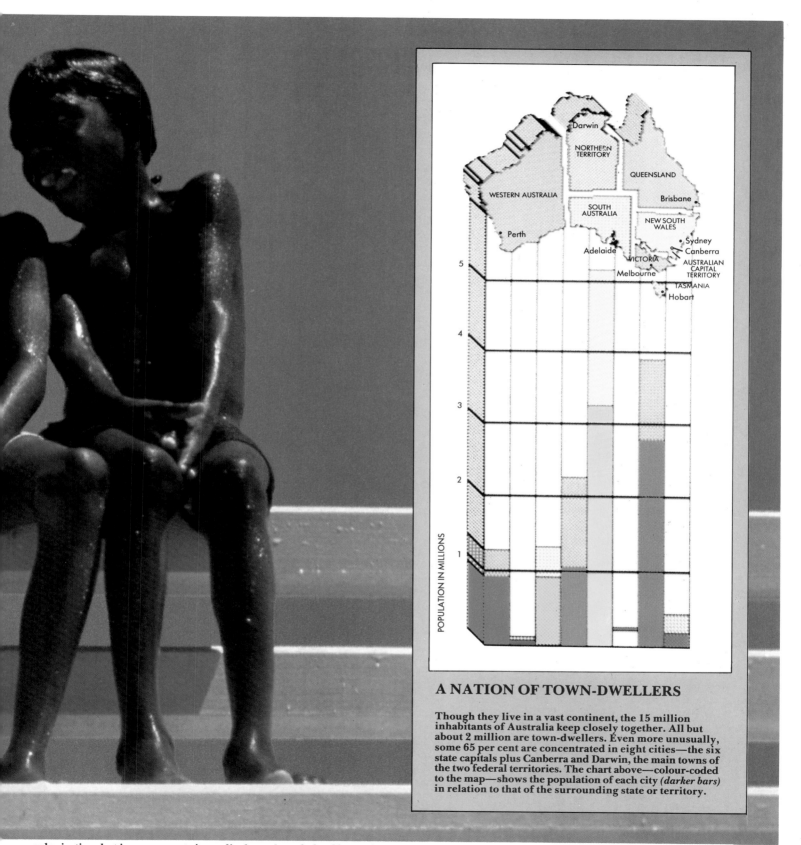

A NATION OF TOWN-DWELLERS

Though they live in a vast continent, the 15 million inhabitants of Australia keep closely together. All but about 2 million are town-dwellers. Even more unusually, some 65 per cent are concentrated in eight cities—the six state capitals plus Canberra and Darwin, the main towns of the two federal territories. The chart above—colour-coded to the map—shows the population of each city *(darker bars)* in relation to that of the surrounding state or territory.

colonization, but improvements in medical care have helped boost the population since World War II to about 200,000.

NEW-FOUND MINERAL WEALTH

Over the past two decades, Australia has emerged as one of the world's major mineral producers. In 1960, minerals accounted for only 7 per cent of the country's exports; by the 1980s, however, the proportion had risen to around 40 per cent. The nation had become the world's largest producer of iron ore, with reserves estimated at 20 billion tonnes.

The continent's energy resources are equally impressive: economists coined the phrase "Lifeboat Australia" to convey the image of a secure, well-stocked refuge riding the stormy waters of international trade and diplomacy. Australia produces almost as much coal as Britain and West Germany, and has unmined reserves put at 30 billion tonnes. Oil production is now running at some 400,000 barrels a day, which provides two thirds of the country's needs. Most of this comes from the offshore Bass Field between Victoria and Tasmania, whose yield is expected to decline sharply by the end of the decade. As a result, exploration is under way to find new fields.

Vast sums and much technical ingenuity are also being expended on tapping Australia's natural gas reserves, which are thought to have greater long-term potential than the crude-oil reservoir. Each mainland state capital is already supplied with piped gas. Current plans are for only about 25 per cent of production to be consumed internally, leaving a large surplus for the export market.

A spectacular sunset casts its glow over fuel tanks on the waterfront at Fremantle, in Western Australia. Described by one 19th-century observer as the

resort of "rogues and drunkards", the port— now part of Perth's metropolitan area—has prospered as Australia's main gateway to the Indian Ocean.

PATTERNS OF LAND USE

More than half of Australia is devoted to rural industries, but only 7 per cent of the land is suitable for intensive use. As the map below shows, the rearing of sheep and cattle, which is possible in relatively dry areas, is widespread; crop farming is largely confined to the moist coastal regions of the south-east and south-west. Tropical fruits and sugar cane are grown in the wet north.

TROPICAL AGRICULTURE

DAIRYING

FORESTRY

MIXED SHEEP AND GRAIN

BEEF CATTLE

MERINO SHEEP

MIXED STOCK RAISING

UNUSED LAND

A flock of hardy Merino sheep troop through a tract of outback scrub used, like 90 per cent of Australia's agricultural land, in its natural state for

low-intensity grazing. Australia has about 15 per cent of the world's sheep, and wool accounts for nearly one tenth of the country's export income.

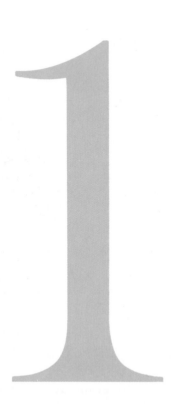

Filling the approach road to the Sydney Harbour Bridge, rush-hour traffic files slowly past the city's world-renowned Opera House. Eighty-five per cent of Australia's 15 million inhabitants live in cities and towns, with an average of nearly one car for every two people.

A COUNTRY COME OF AGE

The first thing that strikes any new-comer to Australia is its size. To a visitor flying in from the north, the low, brown land stretching away almost feature-lessly to the horizon can seem endless, and indeed the distances involved are great. With an area of 7,682,300 square kilometres and a coastline 36,735 kilo-metres long, the country is nearly as large as the continental United States, excluding Alaska. Sydney on the east coast is further from Perth on the west than Madrid is from Moscow.

This massive continent is divided into six states, each with its own elected government with wide responsibility for local affairs. The largest state is Western Australia—four times bigger than Texas and 11 times the size of Great Britain—followed by Queens-land, South Australia, New South Wales, Victoria and the island of Tas-mania. The Australian Capital Terri-tory, a small area surrounding the fed-eral capital Canberra, is directly ruled by central government—as was the sparsely populated Northern Territory until 1978. Now the Northern Territory is a self-governing unit with powers similar to those of the states.

In 1981, the total population of this vast landmass was a mere 15 million, or on average just two people for every square kilometre—less than one tenth the density of the United States and one hundredth that of crowded Great Bri-tain. The reasons for this sparsity lie partly in history. For millennia the con-tinent was inhabited exclusively by an Aboriginal population whose hunter-gatherer lifestyle did not encourage ex-pansion; steady growth only began with the arrival of the first European settlers on the continent in 1788. But even more profound has been the in-fluence of the land itself, whose unique features continue to shape the develop-ment of the nation to the present day.

Australia is the lowest and flattest of continents. More than 50 per cent of the land is less than 300 metres above sea level; a mere 5 per cent rises above 600 metres. It is the driest continent, if exception is made for the uninhabited Antarctica. While the world's land sur-faces receive an average of 72 centi-metres of rainfall each year, Australia's annual precipitation is a niggardly 47 centimetres. This figure, however, is deceptive, because it conceals wide re-gional variations. A few areas such as Tasmania in the south and parts of Queensland in the north are well wa-tered, with up to 400 centimetres of rain; conversely, huge parts of the in-terior and much of the west and central south may suffer drought for years on end, then receive flooding downpours.

The main explanation for Austra-lia's aridity is its position, straddling the 30° line of latitude, where most of the world's deserts in both hemispheres are concentrated. Midway between the equatorial air mass to the north and the polar air mass to the south, Australia is subject to prevalent subtropical high-pressure systems—anti-cyclones—that bring successions of clear, sunny days and raise temperatures in some parts regularly to more than 30°C.

As a result, cloudy days and rainfall can be anticipated with certainty only on the fringes of the landmass. The far north receives summer rains from the edges of the Asian monsoon, while the southern extremities of Australia, both on the east and the west, benefit from winter rains as the sun retreats north of the equator, dragging the northern limit of the wet westerlies after it.

But these winds quickly lose their moisture as they move inland; indeed, in one area of Western Australia, the rainfall declines by almost 2 centi-metres for each kilometre of territory covered. Only rarely does rain reach the centre of the continent where, to quote one small boy's answer to an examination question, "The climate in summer is such that its inhabitants have to live elsewhere."

With so much sunshine, the rain that does fall rapidly evaporates, leaving little water available for human pur-poses. Australia has one great river system, the Murray–Darling, which drains the western slopes of the south-eastern highlands and provides water for large irrigation schemes along its 2,700-kilometre length. Yet in a mere seven days, the River Ganges in India empties into the sea more water than the Murray discharges in a year. The Amazon accomplishes the same task in one and a half days.

A hidden resource helps to alleviate the drought. One seventh of the water available for farming across the nation is buried deep underground in several artesian basins. One of these, the Great Artesian Basin, underlies more than one fifth of the continent north of the Murray and Darling Rivers, making it

1

the largest subterranean reservoir in the world. Although artesian water is too saline for irrigating arable land, it is vital for watering livestock. About 20 per cent of the nation's sheep—from the early days of European settlement a crucial part of the Australian economy—depend on artesian water supplies. More than 30,000 bores have been sunk to exploit this underground treasure; but since the rate of replenishment is slow and demand high, less than 3,000 of them are still in operation. Their outflow makes habitable areas of the continent that would otherwise remain desert, but it does not make them green.

The availability or otherwise of water, more than any other factor, has determined the pattern of Australia's growth, with a populous coastal zone surrounding an interior that is eerily empty. Anyone coming from the congested lands of the developed West cannot fail to be awed by the scarcity of people in certain parts of the country, where neighbours may live several hundred kilometres apart and a trip to

the nearest supermarket or cinema or hospital can entail a round trip of a thousand kilometres or more. This is the outback, whose brown and lonely expanses stretch over much of the Australian interior.

The outback's most prominent feature is the Western Plateau, a low tableland that emerges from Western Australia's coastal plains to cover almost the whole of that state, the greater part of the Northern Territory, much of South Australia and a part of Western Queensland. Some of the plateau is true desert, whether in the form of Sahara-like waves of rippled sand dunes or the more typical, boulder-strewn wildernesses Australians call gibber plains. Rather more of it is semi-desert, a flat, parched tundra dotted with spiky clumps of spinifex grass and mulga and mallee scrub. Here the sun is an enemy and the wind can strike you with the sudden heat of an opened oven door. In its less arid stretches, where rain or artesian bores permit other vegetation to grow, the tundra melds seamlessly into marginal pastureland.

This is the territory of the great cattle stations, farms the size of small kingdoms that can be as much as a million hectares in extent.

Although the average elevation of the plateau is only about 300 metres, the monotony is relieved in widely separated locales by higher ground, notably in the Hamersley Range, whose tallest peak rises about 1,200 metres. Towards the plateau's north-western rim are the irregular ranges of the Kimberley Plateau, a knot of hills about 500 metres high dissected by a maze of short river systems that make this one of the most rugged and inhospitable regions of Australia. Further east are the gentler uplands of Arnhem Land, in the Northern Territory's "Top End", whose main river, the Katherine, drains westwards through a deep, narrow gorge inhabited by freshwater crocodiles. Towards the eastern rim of the plateau are the Macdonnell, Musgrave and Petermann Ranges, which are cut through in places by old river beds and often spectacularly weathered. Alice Springs, whose fame rests

Despite recent immigration from southern Europe and Asia, the faces of a majority of Australia's citizens still reflect British ancestry. Shown here are an army veteran, a spectator at a cricket match, a nickel miner, a sunproofed surfer, a fashionable racegoer and a stockman from the outback.

mainly on its position as one of the world's most isolated modern settlements, grew up around an artesian bore in one such gap in the Macdonnells. From its origins as a station of the Overland Telegraph, built from Darwin to Adelaide in the late 19th century, Alice Springs has developed into a township of over 50,000 people, with a casino and a tourist trade that uses it as a centre for outback travel.

To the east, the plateau comes to an end in a series of low drainage basins extending from the Gulf of Carpentaria in the north to western Victoria in the south. The average elevation of this belt, called the Central Eastern Lowlands, is less than 200 metres, but it falls to more than 10 metres below sea level at Lake Eyre. Heaven help the unwary traveller who expects to find water in this lake or in its tributary rivers, among them Cooper's Creek. Here, the explorers Burke and Wills perished of thirst and malnutrition in 1861 on their return south after making the first south–north crossing of the continent. By a savage irony, nature

has put Australia's biggest lake in the driest part of a dry continent. It has only been known to fill twice this century. Heavy rains in the early 1950s and early 1970s produced a body of water up to 70 kilometres wide and 130 kilometres long, with a brine that was saltier than the sea. Each time, however, the lake was soon reduced to a series of puddles surrounded by thousands of kilometres of salt flats. In 1964, Donald Campbell set a world land speed record on the lake's dry bed.

The Lowlands are rimmed to the east by the Great Dividing Range, which forms an intermittent girdle along the entire length of the continent's flank. With its frequent gaps and an average altitude of under 1,000 metres, it is a barrier to communications only in the south-east, where Australia's highest mountain, 2,228-metre Mount Kosciusko, rises from the section of the range known as the Australian Alps— a major winter sports site containing the mainland's only snow-covered peaks. But the Eastern Highlands, as the range is known to geographers, do

shelter the most complex and varied landscapes in Australia. These include primeval tropical forests in northern Queensland, fantastic pinnacles formed by ancient lavas in the Glasshouse Mountains of southern Queensland, and the deep, ferny gorges and ravines of New South Wales's Blue Mountains—so called because of the bluish atmospheric haze produced by the exudation of oils from the ubiquitous eucalyptus trees.

Almost all of the water that seeps into the Great Artesian Basin and the Murray–Darling river system has its source in the Eastern Highlands. The range provides even more generously on its other, eastern flank, because easterly and south-easterly winds, depositing their moisture on its slopes, make the corridor between the mountains and the sea the best watered and most fertile region of the continent.

Nowhere is this corridor more than 400 kilometres wide, and in places it shrinks to less than 50 kilometres. Yet it is on this narrow fringe, and its continuation along the margins of the south

THE MARSUPIAL MENAGERIE

A koala slumbers trustingly in the fork of a eucalyptus tree.

A baby grey kangaroo peers from its mother's pouch.

A hairy-nosed wombat leaves its burrow to feed in the coolest part of the day.

During Australia's aeons of prehistoric isolation, animal life developed along different lines from the rest of the world. Marsupials—mammals that produce their young in virtually embryonic form and continue to nurture them in the mother's pouch—diversified to fill the evolutionary niches occupied elsewhere by placental mammals.

Today, the commonest marsupials are the kangaroos with some 90 varieties, from the 2.5-metre-high great red kangaroo to the tiny rat kangaroo only 25 centimetres long. Kangaroos live on plants, as do most of Australia's other indigenous animals—in the case of the mild-mannered koala, exclusively on eucalyptus trees. An exception is the carnivorous Tasmanian Devil, a dog-like creature that is no longer found on the mainland.

The duck-billed platypus, an egg-laying aquatic mammal, is quite distinct from the marsupials. Also unique to Australia, it is—along with two types of spiny anteater—one of the only survivors of an otherwise extinct order of mammals.

The quokka is the only kangaroo variety without a long, muscular tail.

A duck-billed platypus glides underwater.

The rare Tasmanian Devil belies its fierce name by its unaggressive manner.

1

coast, that most of the population of the continent is concentrated—about 80 per cent of the people occupying only about 5 per cent of the land. It is here too that the phenomenon of Australian urbanism, as evinced by Sydney, Melbourne and Brisbane as well as such smaller centres as Newcastle and Wollongong, is best studied.

Climate and the availability of water determined that all of Australia's state capitals, including South Australia's Adelaide, Western Australia's Perth and Hobart in Tasmania, would be built on the coast. The marine presence and the proximity of beaches has given them today a unique and enviable ambience of relaxed hedonism. Many office workers structure their lives more or less around the thin yellow lines of sand that fringe the freeways, eagerly accepting early starts to the working day so they can knock off at four in the afternoon in good time for some serious sunbathing on the borders of the boom-

ing surf. One of the archetypal images of today's Australia is of a clutch of teenagers, with sun-bleached hair, blue eyes and the complexions and figures that are the products of affluence, healthy nutrition and open-air living, clustered around a camper-van topped with up-ended surfboards or wind-surfing equipment.

The easy outdoor mood extends to eating and socializing, where it usually takes the form of the great Australian institution, the barbecue. At lunchtime and at dinner, in parks, on beaches and amid the bougainvilleas and gladioli of a hundred thousand suburban gardens, the smell of charred steaks and chops and broiled sausages rises among the hum of smalltalk and the cluster of thirstily downed "tinnies" or beer cans. So popular is barbecueing that concrete broilers, pitted with two or four separate grills, are a common sight in public places. The habit of al-fresco eating also extends to the seafood

stalls in the city streets purveying oysters, crabs, lobsters, mud crabs and yabis—small freshwater crayfish. The beer required to wash down this picnic is kept cool, thanks to another relished convenience, the "Eskie" or polystyrene drink-insulator, which is automatically a part of the luggage for a majority of outdoor excursions.

The pattern of housing in the cities is for the most part extensive rather than concentrated, with a populace spread out around a central business area in often far-flung suburbs. Although flat-dwelling is on the increase, the typical Australian home remains the detached bungalow, with a strip of greenery at the front and a large garden behind. The suburbs have their own focal points in the form of shopping centres, typically built around three sides of a pedestrian precinct. On one side will be the supermarket, on another the post office; boutiques, or perhaps a municipal building or two, will fill the intervening spaces. Many of them incorporate three-storey shopping malls, whose covered passageways serve less to keep off the rain, as is generally true in the Northern Hemisphere, than to act as glass-and-concrete sunshades.

Between them, Australia's six state capitals house some 60 per cent of the population of the country. The reasons why they bulk so large in the nation's life can be traced partly to the nuclear pattern of its growth and the rapid development of highly centralized administration, commerce and transport. Each of the six cities occupies the site where settlement began in its state. At the time, land in the interior was used primarily for grazing rather than for intensive forms of agriculture, so there was little need for the development of large rural centres. Instead, the

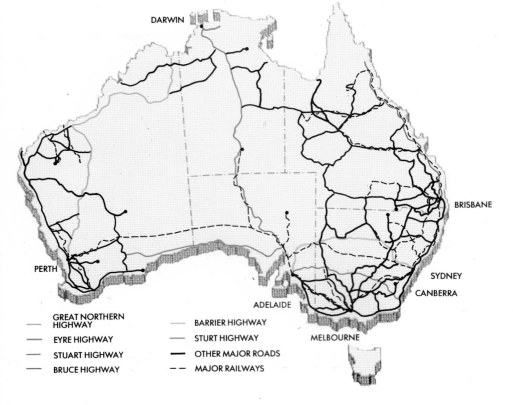

DARWIN

PERTH

ADELAIDE

MELBOURNE

BRISBANE

SYDNEY

CANBERRA

— GREAT NORTHERN HIGHWAY
— EYRE HIGHWAY
— STUART HIGHWAY
— BRUCE HIGHWAY
— BARRIER HIGHWAY
— STURT HIGHWAY
— OTHER MAJOR ROADS
– – MAJOR RAILWAYS

The layout of Australia's major roads and railways indicates the settlement pattern imposed by climate and geography. The arid interior supports only small, isolated towns, while the major cities enjoy the moister, cooler weather of the coastal strip.

produce from each state was funnelled through its capital on the way to markets abroad. In consequence, all the people who were needed to service the trade, from merchants and shippers to bankers and insurance companies, established themselves there. When manufacturing started, the cities were chosen as its logical site; when road and rail networks were built, they inevitably led to and from the capitals. And as the six states became more independent of one another, economic rivalry sprang up between them, so that if one of the capitals expanded, the others tried to emulate it.

Personal inclination has also had a lot to do with the growth of the cities. A traditional Australian saying is "Sydney or the bush", with Sydney and its fellow cities representing affluence and a good time and the bush being equated with discomfort and poverty. In the early days of white settlement, the choice was a real one—to remain in Sydney, and be surrounded by civilized amenities, ready work and social attractions, or to risk carving out a life in the inimical interior, where the promise of an independent lifestyle was counterbalanced by vagaries of drought and flood and a haunting loneliness. Most Australians chose Sydney, and the pattern of urbanization was set for the generations to come.

Sydney is not, of course, the capital of Australia; that honour belongs to Canberra, the city created as the seat of national government after the six states federated in the Commonwealth of Australia on January 1, 1901. But Sydney, with its 3.28 million people spread out over an area of 4,074 square kilometres, is the country's largest and most bustling metropolis. It can also

The provincial calm of Hobart (*above*), capital of the island state of Tasmania, contrasts with the bustle of Melbourne (*top*), Victoria's chief city. Australia's six state capitals were founded within half a century of one another, but each fiercely insists on its individuality.

1

fairly claim to be the oldest, for it was at Sydney Cove, one of the many inlets that indent its beautiful harbour, that Australia's first white settlers came ashore in 1788. The city still centres on the harbour, which the English writer Anthony Trollope described in 1873 as "so inexpressibly lovely that it makes a man ask himself whether it would not be worth his while to move his household goods to the east coast of Australia, in order that he might look at it as long as he can."

Nature ensures that the city still retains its basic glamour, with 30 superb beaches along its eastern edge and an average 6.8 hours of sunshine a day. Yet Sydney also suffers from many of the ailments of rapid and haphazard growth. The shores of Botany Bay, where Captain Cook's ship *Endeavour* dropped anchor in 1770, now shelter polluting heavy industry. Downtown Sydney, framed by those symbols of modern Australia, the Harbour Bridge and the Sydney Opera House, was extensively redeveloped after World War II without any proper consideration for road traffic, with the result that Sydney's one million motor cars thread their way between skyscraper canyons on roads that were never designed to take anything but pedestrians and horses. The cars have also helped to pollute the city; the sun cooks the hydrocarbons produced by the traffic and converts them to a petrochemical smog that now rivals those of Los Angeles and Athens in its noxious intensity.

The most desirable residences in Sydney are the fine houses standing in grounds that front the harbour, while the gentrified 19th-century enclaves of Paddington and Woollahra, with their cast-iron balconies and wooden shutters, have a period charm that is especially popular with the affluent young. But the great majority of Sydneysiders, like the great majority of all Australian city-dwellers, live in the middle and outer suburbs. Give or take a few details, the houses there follow a nationwide pattern, accurately and devastatingly described by the writer Craig McGregor as: "Hundreds of thousands of red-brick bungalows with liver-coloured tile roofs, mass-produced weatherboard houses, fibro cottages with galvanized iron roofs, each set in its own block of land with a lawn out the front and a garden out the back and perhaps a garage along the side, with a picket or brick fence to divide Emoh Ruo from the nature strip and a two-metre paling fence to give some privacy from the Joneses, a motor mower in the laundry, a goblin or kookaburra perched next to the front step, musical door chimes and a street number decorated with a Mexican asleep under his sombrero."

Notwithstanding suburban conformism, Sydney has at least shaken off the unkind title of "the world's smallest large city"—a jibe aimed at the alleged insularity of its citizens. Travel has made many Sydneysiders realize that their city possesses in full measure the mixture of ingredients that distinguishes great metropolises—a homegrown popular culture, a cosmopolitan population, and, alas, organized crime. In recent years, the common talk both in and out of Australia has been that Sydney has suddenly "taken off" by joining the exclusive circle of world centres that act as magnets to attract entrepreneurial energy, high finance and artistic talent.

Separated from Sydney by 900 kilometres of bitumen road and a well-established sense of rivalry, the capital of Victoria, Melbourne, has got the reputation of being more staid than Sydney, more "English". Billy Graham, the American evangelist, said that Melbourne was the most moral city he had visited. A less flattering view was expressed by the actress Ava Gardner, who spent several months in Melbourne shooting the film *On the Beach*, about the after-effects of a nuclear holocaust. She said that it was "a good place to make a film about the end of the world in."

In fact, Melbourne's wide, straight streets, handsome 19th-century buildings and large area of parkland that fringe the central area of skyscrapers give it an air of gentility lacking in Sydney, and its network of electric trams seem pleasantly anachronistic. The city's strait-laced reputation stems less from the urban environment, however, than from its image as the home of the Australian Establishment. From 1901 until 1927, when Canberra became the national capital, it temporarily served as the seat of government. Some federal offices still carry out their functions from Melbourne, and the city remains the headquarters of Australia's main political parties.

Melbourne is the most culture-conscious of Australian cities, housing the nation's leading art gallery—a title under threat from the new National Gallery in Canberra—and most of the small but serious literary and political journals. It is a traditional stamping-ground for Catholic intellectuals and left-wing radicals. It has lovely pubs, and a nightlife that is centred on discotheques, rock venues and eating out, often in BYOG ("Bring Your Own Grog") restaurants. In the 1970s, it was the home of experimental theatres such as La Mama's and the Pram Factory, which spawned a new wave of

Australian playwrights. More importantly for most Melburnians, it is also the main focus of the nation's own brand of football, the 18-a-side Australian Rules, and the scene of the sport's Grand Final, an event that virtually brings the city of Melbourne to a halt for one weekend each September.

Melbourne's image as a bastion of Anglo-Saxon values is somewhat dented by the fact that it is home to more immigrants than any other Australian city; its Greek ethnic population alone exceeds 125,000. At one of the city's high schools, with 1,100 pupils, 90 per cent have an immigrant background, and a single high-rise apartment complex houses people who between them speak a total of 24 different languages. Partly in response to its high immigrant population, Melbourne is very socially minded, having a much wider infrastructure of community groups for the young, the unemployed and other minorities than Sydney.

Brisbane, Australia's third largest city and the capital of Queensland, is less self-important than either Sydney or Melbourne. It has been called the best acclimatized Australian city—a place with its shirt-sleeves rolled up, as befits its semitropical setting. Its atmosphere is matey, easy-going, hospitable, and a little rough around the edges. Even its traditional domestic architecture seems more appropriately Australian than that found in the other cities—timber houses with verandas, raised on stilts to allow cooling air to circulate underneath. The picture has changed in recent years, however. The centre of Brisbane is now skyscraper-modern, and the stilt houses that still remain are sought after by wealthy young couples trying to escape from the alternative accommodation of five-

Guests at the colossal Hilton Hotel in Sydney's city centre take their ease round a lofty rooftop swimming pool. The building boom of the 1960s and 1970s changed the character of the central districts of most of Australia's major cities, with the advent of high-rise office buildings and hotels.

COPING WITH THE SCORCHING SUN

Australians' methods of reconciling the prevailing heat with their predominantly industrious and urban life result in a relaxed style that has become one of the defining characteristics of the nation. The continent's climate ranges from tropical in the far north to cool and temperate in Tasmania. Most of the population, however, is concentrated in the big cities, with average temperatures of between 14 and 20°C, and a reliable five hours or more of sunshine every day. The hottest months are from November to February, when temperatures of over 25°C are common in all the major cities except Hobart.

City-dwellers react to these extremes with some beguiling eccentricities. Some of these are customs in their own right, like the shorn-off uniform adopted by businessmen, who wear shorts and shirt with a tie and city shoes; but others are the improvised tricks of individuals trying to keep cool according to their own ingenuity.

Beer is applied externally to cool one spectator at a cricket match.

A stallholder uses a leafy frill for shade.

A businessman is meticulously correct by Sydney conventions. On Queensland's tourist Gold Coast, a traffic warden matches her pitch.

1

room boxes. The city's reptuation for friendliness has also been tarnished by the poor civil rights record of its state government, particularly with regard to Queensland's Aboriginals.

With a population of about one million, Adelaide, the state capital of South Australia, is a little smaller than Brisbane and very different in mood and layout. It is the best planned of the Australian cities, with a conventional grid plan of single-storey stone bungalows surrounded by a green inner belt of fine parks. In the past it has had a reputation for restraint and careful conservatism. This mood, it is alleged, stemmed from the fact that the city is unique in not tracing its origins to a convict settlement; instead, it was founded by solid Presbyterians full of civic pride and high business ethics. Its traditional image is changing, though. A large-scale programme of industrialization has attracted many migrant workers, and the biennial Adelaide Festival has international recognition as a showplace of the arts. According to Donald Horne, a perceptive analyst of Australian society, Adelaide goes ahead, while Brisbane falls backwards, Sydney falls apart and Melbourne moves forward to stay where it is.

Separated from the rest of urban Australia by several million square kilometres of desert, Perth, the capital of Western Australia, is the most isolated city of its size in the world. Its population of just over 900,000 live some 3,000 kilometres from their nearest metropolitan neighbours in Adelaide. Not surprisingly, the isolation at one time bred a resentment among the people of Perth and Western Australia against the wealthier states of the east. This resentment ran so deep that in 1933 they voted by almost three to one to secede from the Commonwealth of Australia—a move vetoed by London. Since the war, however, the massive mineral wealth of Western Australia has given the city an economic surge that none of the other state capitals can rival. And despite its isolation, Perth has acquired the reputation of being every Australian's second favourite city, renowned for its pleasant blend of urban sophistication and relaxation. It boasts tree-lined streets, uncluttered suburbs and 1,300 square kilometres of parks, nature reserves and open spaces. It also has the Swan River as a focus for leisure and relaxation. An estimated one in three families own boats, giving it quite probably the highest proportion of yachtsmen and small-craft proprietors of any large city in the world.

Most Australian cities grew haphazardly, but Canberra was planned from the start. Although the Australian states federated in 1901, it was eight years before a suitable site was chosen for the new national capital. Unlike the other cities of the east coast, Canberra was to be located inland, on the western slopes of the Eastern Highlands, about 300 kilometres from Sydney and 660 kilometres from Melbourne. A worldwide competition to find a design for the city followed in 1911, which was won by a plan submitted by the American architect Walter Burley Griffin. A further 16 years passed before enough of the city had been constructed for it to take over the duties of federal capital. And it was another 40 years before people took seriously the idea of living in the new capital, as opposed to working in it and going home to Sydney at weekends. Even today, Canberra has the air of an administrative garrison town, with its formal hexagons and crescents adorned by monumental public buildings, foreign embassies and statuary. It is a beautiful city—Australia's "pastoral symphony", as one writer fulsomely described it—which needs the addition of a yeastier population to leaven the mix of civil servants and administrators.

Hobart, capital of Tasmania, started in 1803 with 433 residents, of whom 281 were convicts, and soon grew into a roistering whaling port. Since then it has grown bigger and quieter; as Donald Horne put it, "Hobart started life on the frontier and then went to sleep". But nobody can seriously expect a city of about 170,000 people in a mainly agricultural island state of less than half a million inhabitants to match the frenetic excitement of, say, Sydney—even though two of Australia's eight legal casinos are in Tasmania. Life in Hobart has been described as somewhere between small-town serenity and small-town vindictiveness, but again, that is a mainlander's attitude. Perhaps the kindest thing the rest of Australia can do is to leave the city as it is—standing easy between the blue sea and the deeper blue mountains.

Despite being bombed by the Japanese in 1942 and being flattened twice by cyclones, Darwin—the capital of the Northern Territory—has not only survived but prospered, to become a clean, modern city of some 56,000 people. Where other Australian cities build high, Darwin builds long. Its buildings have few storeys, to resist the cyclones that everybody knows will come again. Darwin's reputation for transience is perpetuated by a floating population of newcomers from other parts of Australia, as well as English, Greek, Chinese, Timorese, Lebanese, Vietnamese, Yugoslav and Italian immigrants—who make it look like a temporary cantonment for exiles in spite of its modern hotels and thriving casino. A sense of isolation and impermanence may be the root cause of its high rate of alcohol consumption—40 per cent above a national average that is itself one of the highest in the world.

Besides the dwellers in these capitals, another quarter of the population live in smaller towns based upon local industries—such as Newcastle, a coal port 100 kilometres north of Sydney; Broken Hill, a town of some 30,000 inhabitants that stands on top of the world's richest known silver, lead and zinc deposits; and Cairns, a tropical Queensland resort town of 40,000, built as the centre of the local cattle and sugar industries, and now achieving importance as a big-game fishing centre popular with well-heeled international sportsmen. A much smaller fraction of Australia's population are scattered in country townships. Parochial and old-fashioned, they often consist of a single main street flanked by weatherboard houses that peter out into the surrounding bushland, and they seem to survive on dreams of their pioneering yesterdays.

More than a million kilometres of roads link Australia's far-flung population centres, of which about half are unsurfaced dirt tracks. Driving itself is more dangerous than in most other developed countries; road death rates are higher per head of population than in comparable countries like the U.S. and Canada, and are twice as high as in Britain—a toll that is blamed primarily on drunken driving.

The state-owned railway system has suffered in the past from the fact that different lines used different gauges, so that until 1969 a journey from the east to the west coast involved at least three

The look of the outback is illuminatingly interpreted in this painting of a bushman in 1890 by Australian artist Arthur Streeton. Streeton was one of the first painters to portray the bush landscape without the romanticized conventions of European rural painting.

1

transfers on to different tracks. This situation is only now being ameliorated by the introduction of a standard rail size. In any case, the continent is so large that, apart from short-range commuting, trains are only suitable transport for the leisured traveller or for bulk commodities such as coal or agricultural produce. The journey from Melbourne to Perth still takes three days. The trip from Adelaide to Alice Springs normally takes slightly less, though on at least one occasion the track was washed away by floods and passengers were rescued by helicopter. The service is picturesquely nicknamed the Ghan—short for Afghan, from the nationality of the camel drivers who once provided the main competition for outback freight transport.

Most Australians travelling between the cities use the domestic air services. In the sparsely populated interior, aircraft not only carry people, but they also supply medical aid through the celebrated Flying Doctor service, help in rounding up livestock, seed and spray crops, and deliver post and library books.

Australians also keep in touch through a nationwide network of telephone, telegraph and postal services. Australian Telecommunications Commission is the country's biggest employer. Because of the huge distances, services are—in theory, at least—tightly stretched. On average, a post office serves 1,110 square kilometres, and in thinly populated Western Australia the figure rises to one for every 4,264 square kilometres.

Like the cities they inhabit, the Australian people have been changing over the past three or four decades, both in their composition and in their self-image. The latter has in the past drawn heavily upon the bush and the tough, wiry, laconic characters supposed to inhabit it. In his penetrating study of the phenomenon, *The Australian Legend*, the historian Russel Ward has drawn a revealing portrait of the ur-Australian, beloved of brochure writers, sentimental politicians and film-makers alike: "According to the myth the 'typical Australian' is a practical man, rough and ready in his manners and quick to decry any appearance of affectation in others. He is a great improviser, ever willing to 'have a go' at anything, but willing too to be content with a task done in a way that is 'near enough'. Though capable of great exertion in an emergency, he normally feels no impulse to work hard without good cause. He swears hard and consistently, gambles heavily and often, and drinks deeply on occasion. Though he is 'the world's best confidence man', he is usually taciturn rather than talkative, one who endures stoically rather than one who acts busily. He is a 'hard case', sceptical about the value of religion and of intellectual and cultural pursuits generally. He believes that Jack is not only as good as his master but, at least in principle, probably a good deal better, and so he is a great 'knocker' of eminent people unless, as in the case of his sporting heroes, they are distinguished by physical prowess. He is a fiercely independent person who hates officiousness and authority, especially when these qualities are embodied in military officers and policemen. Yet he is very hospitable and, above all, will stick to his mates through thick and thin, even if he thinks they may be in the wrong."

The picture projected by this still popular stereotype, as Ward goes on to show, grew out of the lifestyle of a tiny minority of the Australian population: the semi-itinerant workers—such as drovers, stockmen, station-hands and the like—who all earned their living in the outback in the latter part of the 19th and the early years of the present century. The values that the image enshrines are those of a rural proletariat, largely of ex-convict stock, for whom camaraderie, or "mateship" as the Australian version is usually known, was a necessity in the face of a hostile and alien environment. In short, it is a delineation of a class of people about as far removed as it is possible to be from the reality of most Australians' lives today.

Far from being the weatherbeaten bushman of popular imagination, today's Australian belongs to the most urbanized large country on earth. Far from roaming rootlessly, he or she is more likely than his or her counterpart anywhere else in the world to be buying a house; the home ownership figures are higher than 70 per cent. The roving instincts of Australians are now largely confined to the young, who often travel overseas to "see the world" before they return home to settle down to careers and families.

Modern Australian society is predominantly middle class. As late as 1961, there were almost as many blue-collar as white-collar workers in the country—about 1.5 million of each—but since then the number of white-collar jobs has surged ahead. Between the 1961 and 1981 censuses, for example, the number of clerical workers rose by more than half a million, sales workers by a quarter million, and administrative, executive and managerial positions by 110,000. During the same period, the number of farmers and rural workers actually fell by 15,000.

The expansion of a white-collar population is linked to the growth of higher education. In 1939 there were 13,000 university students at six universities; by 1981, the figure had risen to 165,000 at 20 centres of learning. The demand for extra places had partly been fuelled by a post-war baby boom that gave youth an increasing share of the nation's demographic profile. By the early 1980s, more than half the population was under 30 and a third under 20. It is not fanciful to see in the lowering of the age curve one of the motors of the nation's current vitality.

Another fundamental demographic change has been the altering pattern of immigration. Up to the end of World War II, almost all immigrants came from the British Isles, reinforcing the Britishness of Australia's official institutions with their habits of thought, their social customs and their preconceptions. New arrivals could feel at home in a country where they could drive on the left and pay for things in pounds, shillings and pence (the Australian dollar dates only from 1966, when the currency was decimalized). The nation's institutions were equally close to those of the mother country. Not only were the laws strictly after the British pattern, but judges wore the same archaic paraphernalia of robes and wigs. Children could be educated, if their parents wished, in fee-paying independent schools, and the universities were as British as their founders and staff could make them.

But it was in the details of daily life that the British flavour of pre-war Australia became most apparent. A culture that had evolved in a cold, wet, northern climate was thrown into high relief when imported lock, stock and barrel

A woman hangs a pushchair on hooks provided for the purpose before boarding a bus in Perth, the capital of Western Australia. The trams that were a feature of Australian cities from the 19th century on have for the most part been replaced by civic bus services.

into the sunny light of the subtropical south. The working day in those times still generally started at the British hour of 9.00 a.m., when the sun was already blazing. Few people dared suggest that a Mediterranean timetable would be more comfortable, and that it would make better sense to start in the cool of the day and stop earlier—or else later, allowing for the restful interposition of a lunchtime siesta.

The clothes normally worn showed the same loyalty to ancestral conventions and disregard of convenience: dark suits with waistcoats, collars and ties, sensible dresses. Eating habits were equally hidebound, focusing on incongruous, hot, meat-and-two-veg

dinners. Such traditionalism reached its apotheosis at Christmastime, when roast turkey and plum pudding were solemnly served in the best Dickensian manner under the sweltering heat of the high Australian summer.

Attitudes began to change in the course of the war. The shock of the Japanese threat, including the bombing of Darwin, led to a rethinking of attitudes that was to affect profoundly the structure of Australian society and ultimately to reduce the British influence. Politicians of all colours came to the conclusion that the continent was dangerously underpopulated, and had insufficient forces to defend itself. A policy of financially assisting immi-

1

grants with the costs of passage was adopted, and it was extended to settlers from continental Europe as well as from Britain. The result was a massive influx of almost 3 million newcomers, arriving at an average of 100,000 a year, until restrictions were again imposed in late 1974. By that time the proportion of Australians born overseas had doubled, from one in 10 to one in five. Fewer than one third of the new arrivals came from Britain; Italy provided about 16 per cent, Greece about 10 per cent, with Germany and the Netherlands also contributing substantial numbers.

The most recent trend has been a vast increase in the number of Asian immigrants. Since the 1950s, the infamous "White Australia" policy, used in effect to disbar Asian entry, has been gradually eroded. By the early 1980s, roughly a third of all immigrants were Asian, and the "Asianisation" of the country was an issue beginning to arouse political passions.

The changing structure of Australian society is reflected in the shifting pattern of religious allegiance. In 1933, nearly 40 per cent belonged to the Church of England, and about 20 per cent—mainly of Irish ancestry—were Catholic; most of the remaining population was affiliated to other Protestant denominations. Yet by the mid-1980s, the number of Catholics—swollen by immigration from the Mediterranean countries—was rivalling the Anglican total, and some 3 per cent of the population were Greek Orthodox. A growing number were churchless; whereas in 1933 only one Australian in 500 claimed to have no religion, almost 10 per cent of the population now avowed no religious allegiance.

Although tolerance prevails for the most part, Australia has not been completely immune to religious discrimination. Until the 1960s, for instance, Jews were denied entrance to the Melbourne Stock Exchange, and Catholics were rarely granted admittance to the exclusive clubs that cater for the financial and farming élites. Polarization of a less harmful kind is also apparent in politics, with Roman Catholics providing the backbone of support for the Australian Labor Party and, to an even greater extent, the Democratic Labor Party, a breakaway group that split off in the 1950s over the issue of Communist infiltration of trade unions, who have traditionally been the A.L.P.'s chief backers. Conversely, Presbyterians and Methodists give strong support to the Liberal Party, the nation's main right-of-centre grouping, and to the conservative National Country Party, the mouthpiece of rural voters. The country's other main political party, the Democrats, occupies the political middle ground, and plays an important role in holding the balance between the parties of the right and left.

Religious differences also help account for the fact that in Australia, a country whose six states each operate a free public education system, about one fifth of the primary schools and one quarter of the secondary schools are private, fee-paying establishments. Some 80 per cent of the private schools are Catholic foundations. Most of the remainder are run on the English boarding-school model, and are either Anglican or Presbyterian in their religious affiliation. In terms of places won at Australia's universities, these private schools undoubtedly do better than the state schools.

Heated debates about the wisdom of giving Australians the choice between competing educational systems have not deterred recent immigrants from setting up their own private schools, dedicated to the preservation of minority cultures and languages. In fact, many of these establishments receive funds from the government, reflecting Australia's shift away from a policy of assimilation to one of multiculturalism or ethnic pluralism. In 1983, for example, Sydney's first full-time Greek school opened with an enrolment of 600 pupils and a three-year waiting list. In the same year, Australian Jews were operating 14 schools, including Victoria's Mount Scopus College, claimed to be the world's largest Jewish secondary school outside Israel itself, with 2,300 students. There was a full-time Spanish-language school in Canberra, a Japanese school near Sydney, a school in Sydney's western suburbs run by Hmong refugees from the mountains of Laos, and a gypsy school teaching Romany in Perth.

In appearance, then, the traditional view of the Australian as described by Russel Ward has long been consigned to the junkyard of legend. Yet, like many another cherished myth, it remains, in spite of all logic, unreasonably prevalent—so prevalent, indeed, that the observer ends up wondering whether, in spite of all evidence to the contrary, it might not still contain a grain of truth. Certainly, the realities of life in modern suburban Australia hardly square with that tough, bushman image. Yet perhaps just through force of repetition and some deep desire in the national subconscious for the claim to be true, the picture retains a real force. Although the conditions that created the lifestyle have disappeared, the approach to life it summarizes re-

DELICATE TRACERIES OF IRON

Houses in many hot countries are built with verandas and balconies to provide shade. In Australia's cities, however, these architectural devices are often given a special character by the traceried ironwork of which they are constructed.

In the mid-19th century, when Australian towns were expanding rapidly, iron was cheap and local taste ran to florid patterns. The wedding-cake fussiness of typical 19th-century work later fell from favour—indeed, in the 1940s many fine examples were destroyed—but the older districts of certain cities, such as Paddington in Sydney and Melbourne's Carlton, still have buildings that strike a welcome note of frivolity among the usually utilitarian architecture.

Tracery shrouds a Queensland hotel.

A balcony on slender pillars casts lacy shadows on the walls of a house in Melbourne.

1

mains the most distinctively Australian feature of the continent's inhabitants to this day.

Australia began as a derivative culture, settled by Europeans centuries later than most of the New World, and it is still one today. Its bush is characterized by barbed wire and galvanized iron, products of the machine age of European civilization; its cities by skyscrapers and commercialism, products of the American age. The unique creation of Australian culture is to be found elsewhere: in a social ethos which, in spite of decades of affluence and high-pressure ways of thinking and living, has survived in modified form to the present day.

A large part of that ethic has to do with egalitarianism: the idea that every person should be, or at least act, equal. The English novelist D.H. Lawrence noticed it when he came to Australia to write his novel *Kangaroo*: people there might feel "better off" than others but not "better", he wrote. Generations of immigrants from Britain and other more status-conscious countries have commented on how informal and free from snobbery Australia appears to be.

This openness should not be confused with an absence of distinctions of class or wealth, which have been increasing with the nation's post-war affluence. But in its social conventions Australia remains determinedly democratic. Taxi drivers may still take offence if clients do not sit in the front of the car; tipping is less prevalent than in most Western countries; perfect strangers will call you "mate" and invite you into their homes. According to Donald Horne, writing in 1964, "If a Russian aristocrat of 1917 could see photographs of Australia now, he might assume that it was here that the people had taken over, not Russia."

The characteristic Australian ethos also has something to do with character signals, such as friendliness. This is a modern descendant of "mateship", which was an exclusively male ritual; today you would have to add "sisterhood". Male and female, there is less of a sense of enclosure about the people than in, say, England or France or Sweden. On country roads in Australia people still nod or wave to each other when they pass, even if they are complete strangers. The same can happen on the beaches along the coast, or in town at bus stops or in lifts; it is an acknowledgement of commonality which nobody would think of providing in, say, New York.

To understand Australia, the observer must search in the everyday habits of everyday people, for if ever there was a nation in which the pattern of life was dominated by the majority of the population rather than by a few individuals or an élite, it is Australia today. One reason for this lack of pomp is the comparative brevity of white Australian history, which means that grand institutions and grand traditions have had less time to establish themselves than in older nations. Another factor is an Australian habit of "cutting the tall poppies down to size"—the tall poppies including anyone who is more than averagely successful—and, in the words of the bush-balladeer Henry Lawson, making sure that the rich and powerful get "educated down". This tendency is less common now, because Australia has become more status-conscious and competitive in the post-war years; but the social force of the common people remains formidable.

Finally, to come to terms with that which is most characteristic of Austra-

lian life, you must look outside the daily pattern of work. Work is not unimportant, but the general trends of employment—the shift away from the farm and towards the office, the movement of a large proportion of married women into the labour force—tend to be similar in most developed nations. It is what people do outside of working hours that most distinguishes one country from another, and in Australia leisure counts. There is an old, pervasive feeling that life is not made for work but for living. A South Pacific hedonism runs through the culture, tempting Brisbane office workers into the park for a longer-than-legal lunch of salad and beetroot sandwiches, luring truant schoolboys into the adults-only movie in the Kings Cross district of Sydney, leading surfers to drift up and down the east coast in search of the unattainably perfect wave, drawing counter-culture drop-outs to lead an imitation Aboriginal life in communes and co-operatives in the subtropical mountains to the north, and in colder Victoria bringing 100,000 roaring partisans to the Australian Rules grand final in the Melbourne Cricket Ground. All in their different ways are engaged in the time-honoured pursuit of having a good time. Because a life of leisure, and not just for the leisured classes, continues to be what much of the Australian dream is all about.

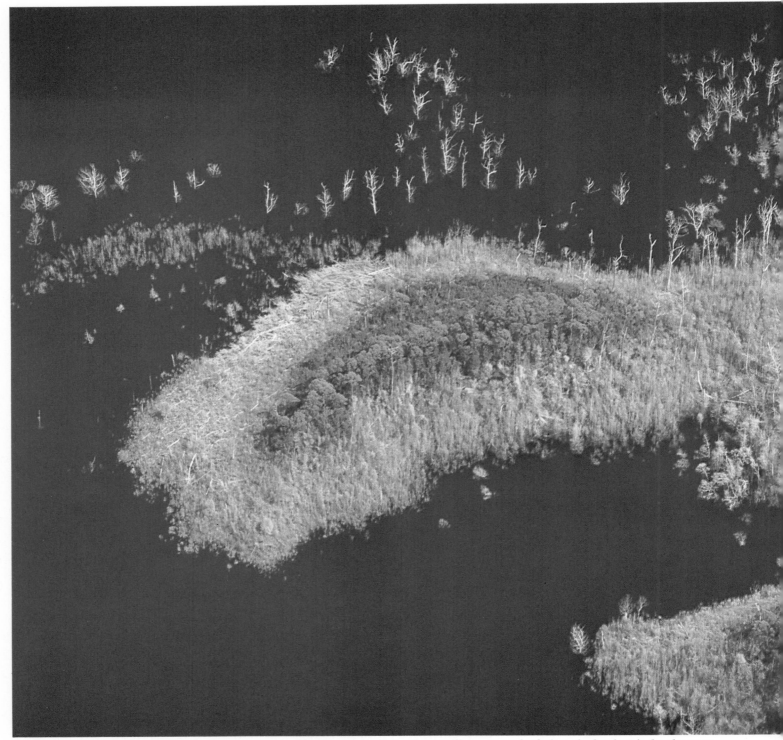

The skeletons of hundreds of trees rise from the waters of Tasmania's Lake Gordon, swollen as a result of a huge hydroelectric development.

IMAGES OF AN ARCHAIC LAND

Australia is the driest and flattest of continents. Over great tracts of the interior—remote from the sea, desiccated and crumbled to dust by the relentlessly blazing sun—less than 25 centimetres of rain falls a year. Most of the lakes and rivers that feature on maps of these regions were formed in a long-past, wetter geological era, and are now only occasionally filled by rare cloudbursts. During aeons of geological silence, mountain ranges that once rose ruggedly from the plains have worn down to rounded stubs.

Yet no continent the size of Australia could fail to offer a variety of scenery. There may be few mountains that reach conspicuous heights, but rivers fed by the moisture-laden Pacific trade winds have cut romantic gorges through the Great Dividing Range on the eastern seaboard. Further south, in the cool, damp island state of Tasmania, lakes nestle amid tree-clad slopes. Most spectacularly of all, the nation's 36,735-kilometre shoreline boasts a catalogue of splendours ranging from the surf-lined paradise of the southern strands to the fantastical coral wilderness of the Great Barrier Reef off the Queensland coast.

In Tasmania's Central Highlands, a placid Lake Dove lies beneath the twin peaks of Cradle Mountain amid forests of pine and eucalyptus. The deep lakes of the island state were gouged out during the last ice age 20,000 years ago, when Tasmania was still joined to the mainland.

LAKES SUCKED DRY BY THE SUN

After rare rains, saline water fills South Australia's Lake Everard. It will soon evaporate, leaving a salt-pan almost as parched as the sand dunes.

Dunes nicknamed "the Walls of China" border the bed of Lake Mungo in New South Wales, dry for 16,000 years.

THE UBIQUITOUS EUCALYPTUS

An avenue of hardy river gums, nourished by water stored in their leathery leaves, lines the dry bed of the Todd River near Alice Springs in the Northern Territory. The low rainfall of the outback ensures that the stream rarely flows.

Elegant karri trees, a type of eucalyptus that can reach 75 metres, tower over the luxuriant verdure of the Warren River valley in the south-west corner of Western Australia. Heavy rainfall and high humidity make this the only area of the massive state to support such dense vegetation.

Corrugated ridges of the Macdonnell Ranges run for over 320 kilometres across the Northern Territory, enclosing parallel valleys peppered with ghost gums. These are among the most ancient mountains on earth, eroded over 400 million years by the elements and old water courses.

Dawn mist gathers in the valleys of the Blue Mountains, a section of the Great Dividing Range 100 kilometres west of Sydney. Rivers and streams have dissected this sandstone plateau to create a dramatic, fertile area of precipitous gorges, escarpments and peaks over 1,000 metres high.

Minerals stain the massive granite
boulders on Wilson's Promontory,
the southernmost point of the
Australian continent, 200 kilometres
south-east of Melbourne. This
rugged, hook-shaped headland,
sculpted by sea and wind, was joined
to Tasmania until the sea cut off the
bridge 8,000 years ago.

Motor-boats linger around one of the
innumerable sandy cays that, together
with larger atolls and islands, form
the Great Barrier Reef. The 2,000
kilometres of coral chain is formed
chiefly of the limestone casings of
billions of tiny marine animals called
polyps, accumulated over 15,000 years.

COPYRIGHTED SEP 3 1888.   THE CITY OF SYDNEY

EMERGING FROM A COLONIAL PAST

A print of 1888 shows the city of Sydney 100 years after its foundation as a British penal colony. Possessing one of the finest harbours in the world, the settlement soon became a focus of trade and shipping, and by the time of its centenary it had developed into a thriving metropolis of 350,000 people.

More than 35,000 years ago, the first settlers arrived in Australia. They came from South-East Asia, and for the most part they walked. A great ice age had lowered the level of the waters, and a fragile land bridge extended through what are now Indonesia and New Guinea to the empty southern continent. We do not know how long they spent on their journey, whether it was an epic or an ordeal, or whether they even knew that they were making it. Like every human being at the time, they were hunter-gatherers, foraging in small bands; they may have fled in haste from violent neighbours or idly meandered after game and wild fruits, taking generations in the crossing.

Then, many thousands of years after their first arrival, the massive ice caps of the last great glaciation thawed, and the waters rose once more. Tasmania was cut off from the mainland, and of the great land bridge to Asia only a scattering of islands, swept by perilous new seas, remained. For the people of Australia, a long age of peaceful isolation began.

Their continent, however, was not a paradise. The same climatic changes that had isolated it from the rest of the world had stricken much of it with perpetual drought, and few areas offered an easy living. Like all hunter-gatherers, they were semi-nomadic and ranged over vast tracts of territory to make the most of a scanty food supply. Materially, they had few possessions, and no weapon was more advanced than a stone-tipped wooden spear or the curious throwing stick they called a boomerang; except in the cooler, southern regions, they rarely troubled to make clothing.

Culturally, though, their lives were rich and complex. Over the quiet, uncharted centuries, they developed a marvellous web of totems and taboos that not only allowed them to harvest the frugal necessities of life from an often forbidding environment, but also provided intense spiritual satisfaction. Everything was magical; but it was usually a magic based upon acute observation of the natural world. Everything was part of the whole. A man could see his ancestors in a rock or a star, or in a kangaroo upon a far horizon. A whole people lived in a state of permanent communion with the world about them, transcending birth and death and time itself. That timeless lifestyle lasted for millennia and, undisturbed, might have lasted for millennia more. But only distance and the ocean protected it; half a world away, in Europe, a very different kind of people, aggressive and ambitious, were finding how easily distance could be abolished.

Possibly others had probed towards Australia before the European explorers made their first landfalls. The Incas of Peru, for instance, told their Spanish conquerors of a great expedition of theirs to a fabulously interesting southern land. Less fancifully, some modern

2

Chinese historians have claimed that in the sixth century B.C. their mariners had made the crossing from the Indonesian archipelago. A few fragments of Chinese ceramics—though of a much later date—have been found on Australia's northern coasts. Macassar fishermen from Indonesia, in search of the delicacy known as bêche-de-mer, a form of large sea-cucumber, are known to have been regular visitors. But the northern and north-western shores, the most likely point of contact for venturesome Asian navigators, are unwelcoming. No permanent settlement was ever attempted in that area.

The European idea of a great southern continent can be traced back to the geographers of classical times, who theorized that an antipodes must exist to counterbalance the landmass of Eurasia. Since they also theorized that the equator was an impenetrable, fiery barrier, that seemed to be the end of the matter. Nevertheless, *Terra Australis Incognita*, the unknown southern land that was first proposed by the second-century Greek philosopher Ptolemy and then adopted by his Roman successors, continued to fascinate educated men. By the time the Portuguese launched the great age of exploration in the 15th century, its existence—although entirely unproved—was more or less undoubted.

The sea-routes opened by the Portuguese round Africa to India and beyond made nonsense of the idea of an impassable equator. By the early 16th century, they were sailing and trading as far east as Java, and mapping the northern coast of New Guinea. But despite tantalizing hints that they may have touched on the Australian mainland, there is still no firm evidence of discovery. The wealth they brought

back, however, attracted others to explore the same far-off waters.

The Spanish made the next contribution. In 1606, Luis Váez de Torres traversed the dangerous shoals of the strait that now bears his name, passing south of New Guinea and within a few kilometres of the Australian coast. But

Torres' feat went without public recognition for almost 150 years; fearful of competition from European rivals, the authorities in Madrid kept his report strictly secret.

Their fear was understandable, because others were also at large in the Pacific. In the same year that Torres

A portrait of 1776 *(left)* shows the English explorer, Captain James Cook, shortly before the voyage that was to end with his death at the hands of natives in Hawaii. Six years earlier, Cook had sailed his ship, *Endeavour (below)*, to Australia's east coast, blazing a trail for British settlement.

completed his voyage, a Dutch ship under the command of Willem Janszoon, nosing around New Guinea in search of gold, made the first definite European landfall in Australia, on the desolate Cape York Peninsula.

The Dutch were traders *par excellence*, commercial leaders in Europe itself and, in the early 17th century, they were busily creating a lucrative mercantile empire based on Java. Unlike the Spaniards, they had no interest in glory: their purposes were much more down to earth. As an official of the Dutch East India Company, founded in 1602, declared, "With God's aid, we may obtain some great booty in the South Seas." Exploration was frowned upon unless the commercial benefits were clear. Yet almost despite themselves, the Dutch contrived to map nearly half the Australian coast, and they gave the continent its first European name, New Holland.

They were not much impressed by what they saw. Reports and ships' logs are almost unanimous: "In our judgement, this is the most arid and barren region that could be found anywhere on earth," wrote one captain in 1623; another, who was shipwrecked on the north-western coast in 1629, declared the continent "an accursed earth".

Its inhabitants were even less appealing. Abel Tasman, who between 1642 and 1644 had commanded two expeditions grudgingly financed by the Company's merchants, described them as "naked, beach-roving wretches, miserably poor . . . and in many places of a very bad disposition". The English explorer-pirate William Dampier, who landed on the coast of north-west New Holland in 1688, was even more damning: "They have the most unpleasant looks and the worst features of any people that I ever saw, though I have seen great variety of savages."

Sadly, no one recorded what the "savages" thought of their visitors: blotchy white, scurvy-ridden, womenless men, with their floating islands of wood and cord and creaking canvas, their bizarre, sweat-soaked garments, their terrible weapons and their ignorant disdain of sacred places. Still, they were few in numbers, and in some of the early violent encounters it had been discovered that they could be killed. It would have been a perceptive Aboriginal indeed who realized at the time that his people's long sway over their arid land, counted once in tens of thousands of years, would now be measured out in decades.

For a while, however, it seemed as if the Europeans had gone away and for-gotten all about them. The Dutch were not interested in colonies, even if they had felt New Holland might support them; Spain and Portugal had enough to handle with their existing empires; and the rising powers of Britain and France spent much of the 17th and most of the 18th century at war with one another. Besides, the South Pacific was simply too far away, so the barrier of distance still held.

For more than a century after Tasman's voyages, the eastern coast of Australia remained unmapped. By the 1760s, though, both Britain and France were probing cautiously into the Pacific, partly lured by the old legends of *Terra Australis Incognita*, partly inspired by the scientific curiosity of an age that prided itself on its enlightenment, and perhaps also, in Britain's case, influenced by the capture of ancient Spanish and Portuguese charts of the area during the Seven Years' War.

In 1770, Captain James Cook, the greatest Pacific navigator of all time, discovered the eastern shore. He mapped it with the painstaking accuracy for which he was famous, and brought back to Europe the first glowing report of the new land. Around the anchorage he named Botany Bay, after the variety of botanic specimens he found there, he reported "a deep black soil", producing "as fine a meadow as ever was seen". Cook also put in the first good word for the land's people, despite the fact that they had greeted his arrival with a volley of spears. "They may appear to some to be the most wretched people on Earth," wrote the explorer, "but in reality they are far happier than we Europeans . . . They sleep as sound in a small hovel or even in the open as the King in his Pallace *(sic)* on a Bed of Down." Neverthe-

2

This painting of *erythrina vespertilio*, an Australian flower, was sketched by Sydney Parkinson, an artist who sailed with Captain Cook on his historic voyage of 1770. Parkinson died of typhoid on the journey home and many of his botanical drawings were later coloured in by an artist in England.

less, after the manner of the times, Cook judiciously took possession of the eastern half of the continent, naming it New Wales to distinguish it from New Holland far to the north-west.

Cook's reports were received with interest back home, but the British government could muster little enthusiasm for new colonies. The existing ones were trouble enough; in 1775, the long, nagging quarrel with the American colonists erupted into a full-scale war of independence, and Britain went on to suffer one of her most humiliating defeats. The idea of risking the same kind of debacle in Cook's New Wales sent shudders down official spines.

Yet in the end, it was precisely the defeat in America that brought about the first white settlement in Australia. What was to be done with the American colonists who had remained loyal to the crown? Surely, pamphleteers argued, the British government owed them something, and what better way of repaying debts than to settle them in the South Seas, where they would deservedly prosper as well as providing Britain with a bastion of power in the Pacific? In principle, the government agreed. But the loyal Americans were far away, and at home the government faced a problem at once more sordid and more pressing.

For over a century, America had served as a dumping-ground for convicted British criminals. But the new United States would have none of them, and since the beginning of the transatlantic war, the wretches had been accumulating by the thousands in overcrowded prison hulks anchored in Portsmouth and the Thames River. Not only were the hulks a menace to health, even by the standards of an unhygienic age, but every convict held

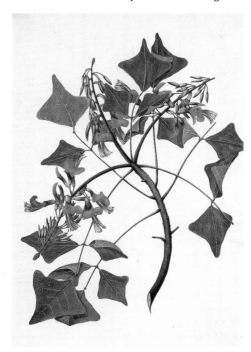

there cost His Majesty the shocking sum of £27 per annum.

To money-conscious British bureaucrats, Australia began to seem like a promised land. Not only would it absorb the inmates of Britain's jails, but with a little luck, and taking Cook's survey reports at their most optimistic reading, an Australian settlement could provide the British Admiralty with a source of timber and other naval supplies. It could serve as a base for whaling in southern waters and as a port of call for Pacific traders, and it would discourage French naval activity in the region. If the convicts worked hard and rehabilitated themselves, so much the better. If not, they would be too far away to do much harm.

Orders were issued. In 1787, 772 miserable and terrified convicts—568

men, 191 women and 13 unfortunate children—were prodded under armed guard into the holds of 11 transports in Portsmouth harbour, and blacksmiths quickly chained them to the walls. On May 13, the convoy, complete with retinue of seamen and of Royal Marines to guard the prisoners, set sail; and on January 18, 1788, the ships dropped anchor in the empty silence of Botany Bay. For most of their involuntary passengers, it seemed little enough cause for celebration. But nevertheless, their huddle of stinking transports would be immortalized as Australia's First Fleet. The roaring of the anchor cables through the ships' hawse-holes shattered the tranquillity of the Bay; it also marked the end of a continent's long and peaceful sleep, and announced the birth of the new nation.

It could scarcely have been born in less auspicious circumstances. The place did not match Cook's eulogies. Instead of the promised "meadows", the new arrivals found only a sandy wilderness. So unpromising was the original landing-site in Botany Bay that the fleet within a few days moved on to the next harbour to the north, named Port Jackson by Cook but soon rechristened Sydney. The soil was better there, but even so, the task of cultivating the virgin land was a challenge to tax even an expert. And the convicts of the First Fleet were anything but expert.

It is a fond Australian myth that the nation's founding fathers were a mixture of free-thinking political prisoners and stalwart poachers, who were condemned by brutal and repressive British laws. True, the laws were savage. Most of the convicts had been found guilty of offences a more enlightened age would have regarded as trivial, and

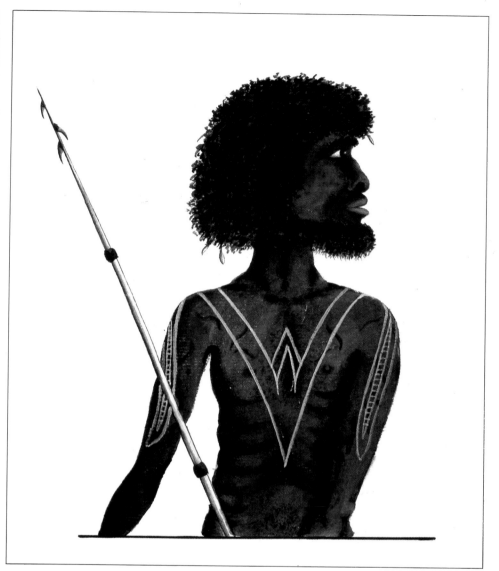

the colony's log book of their crimes, matched generally with a sentence of seven years' transportation, makes pathetic reading: "Picking Pockets"; "Privately Stealing"; "Shoplifting"; or simply "Misdemeanour". (Most of them were lucky to have escaped the hangman's rope.) But there were no politicals and very few poachers among them. The majority, in fact, were urban petty criminals, completely lacking in farming experience. And since they had been selected from Britain's crowded jails by officials eager to rid themselves of their most troublesome—or simply most useless—inmates, the convicts were unpromising material even for a force of unskilled labourers.

That the colony survived at all, let alone prospered, was largely thanks to one man, its governor, Captain Arthur Phillip. A regular naval officer, Phillip had already demonstrated his professional skills by bringing the First Fleet, intact and reasonably healthy, to Australia. Now he used skills of a different order, alternately bullying with the lash and cajoling with supplies of Royal Navy rum until some semblance of a settlement was created. But it was an uphill struggle. Even the colony's tools were "the worst that ever was seen," as Phillip wrote despairingly to London. And he got little help from the soldiers and the marines supposedly under his command. Their officers "declined any interference with the convicts" and lived as much as possible a separate existence. For two years London ignored Phillip's complaints, and when, in 1790, the first ships from home appeared, they brought another batch of convicts to add to his troubles.

For the first few years, the colonists were almost entirely dependent on food supplied from overseas, and at times

the colony were perilously close to starvation. Gradually, though, more and more land came under cultivation, and by the time ill-health forced Phillip's recall to England in 1792, the land now known as New South Wales was nearly self-supporting. The first landowners were time-served soldiers and sailors, and convicts whose sentences had expired. They were granted title by the governor, who also used his power to create a new class of "emancipists"—

convicts who were given a conditional pardon as a reward for good behaviour. Emancipists were forbidden to return to England until their period of transportation was over, but otherwise enjoyed most of the rights of free men.

Slowly and painfully, they built the colony up. Sydney grew from a collection of crude huts to a scruffy but thriving little town, and isolated settlements sprang up in a hinterland that went as far as the Blue Mountains, which in the

early 19th century were regarded as an impassable barrier to westward expansion. Subsidiary convict settlements were built at Port Phillip, close to the modern city of Melbourne, in 1803—a short-lived experiment—and in the following year at Hobart and Launceston in Van Diemen's Land, as Tasmania then was known.

If free settlers were still reluctant to risk their futures so far from home, the British law courts continued to supply convicts in plenty. For the first time, they included a significant number of political offenders: in 1798 a failed rebellion in Ireland yielded about 1,200 embittered immigrants. Some of them staged another unsuccessful rising near Sydney in 1804; in the years to come, the Irish and their descendants would provide a noisily anti-British section of the population that helped to counterbalance misty-eyed sentiment about the Mother Country.

The most interesting early development, though, came not from the prisoners but from their guards. The New South Wales Corps was not, to put it mildly, the most distinguished unit in the British Army. After a couple of years, however, they began to show a remarkable commercial acumen. They realized their pay amounted to most of the colony's money supply, and used their power to create an unbreakable trading monopoly—especially in rum, for which demand always exceeded supply. Soon they were able to transfer their profits into land, radically altering the future shape of the colony.

Originally, the plan had been to create a self-supporting society: free settlers and emancipists were to receive small grants of land and to be left on their own. But the land was poor, and so were its new owners. Unable to im-

Shown in a 19th-century illustration, British convicts sail in cages to far-off Australia *(top).* Such shipments continued from 1787 to 1868, by which time 160,000 men, women and children had been transported. As the sample "passenger list" *(above)* shows, even shoplifting could lead to exile.

prove it, or even to buy the livestock that could provide essential manure, they soon went bankrupt and sold out to the officers, who thus acquired vast and reasonably profitable estates. The concentration of land and wealth increased even more when sheep were introduced, first for their meat and then, more lucratively still, for their wool. And when a governor—Captain Bligh, the celebrated victim of the *Bounty* mutiny of 1789—tried to halt the process, his officers arrested and deposed him in 1808 for "tyranny". It seemed likely that the future Australia would be a country ruled by a tiny minority of powerful landowners, dominating a landless, poverty-stricken population.

But such a fate was not to be. The home government, finally shocked into action by Bligh's sequestration, sent an energetic new governor, Lachlan Macquarie, with a regiment of fighting men, and the New South Wales Corps was disbanded. Under the new regime, prosperity grew. Enterprising seamen, many of them ex-convicts, won wealth from sealing and whaling.

Nor was the little, settled strip of New South Wales any longer all of Australia. In 1813, the Blue Mountains were crossed for the first time, and excited explorers returned with tales of endless good grazing land. Just as important, there were enough colonists to settle them. As late as 1820, there were still only 1,307 free immigrants; but reports were reaching London of emancipists who had made huge fortunes and been accepted by Macquarie as rehabilitated citizens, and Australia was at last being considered as a good place to send Britain's excess population, not just its criminals.

Nor were the newcomers restricted to New South Wales. In 1829, Britain, which had formerly laid claim to only the eastern half of Australia, chose to extend its dominion to the entire continent, mainly to pre-empt European rivals with an interest in the area. New settlements were by then springing up. A further penal colony had been established on the Brisbane River about 1,000 kilometres north of Sydney in 1824. The first convictless settlement was founded near present-day Perth, in Western Australia, in 1829, followed by a colony near Melbourne in 1835. When Adelaide followed suit in 1836, all six future capitals of the present-day states were in rudimentary existence.

All of these communities were on or near the coast, so that they could be supplied by water. The opening-up of the interior of the continent was a more challenging matter altogether, and it fell to a courageous band of adventurers to make the pioneering journeys on which all further expansion depended. As early as 1829, Charles Sturt had set off from Sydney in an attempt to trace the southern river system to a hoped-for inland sea. The sea turned out to be illusory, but Sturt did discover enough good land to encourage the subsequent opening-up of South Australia. A Scottish officer, Major Thomas Mitchell, discovered another vast area of good land in south-eastern Australia in 1836. Christened Australia Felix by its discoverer, it was to be the nucleus of the future state of Victoria. Less fortunate was 25-year-old Edward Eyre. In 1840,

A CHRONOLOGY OF KEY EVENTS

c. 35,000 B.C. The earliest Aboriginals appear in Australia, arriving across a land bridge from South-East Asia. For thousands of generations the Aboriginals live a finely balanced hunter-gatherer's life, dispersed in family groups over the continent.

1606 Willem Janszoon, a Dutch mariner, sails into the Gulf of Carpentaria, becoming the first European to land on the continent. In the next 30 years, Dutch navigators manage to chart much of the northern and western coastline, naming the territory New Holland.

1642 The Dutch explorer Abel Tasman reaches Tasmania, mistaking it for the southern coastline of New Holland.

1770 Captain James Cook, the British explorer, lands in Botany Bay (now part of Sydney). He claims the whole eastern seaboard of Australia for Britain, naming it New Wales.

1788 Given the task of establishing a penal colony by the British government, Captain Arthur Phillip *(above)*, in command of the First Fleet, arrives with about 1,000 settlers, more than half of them convicts. Attracted by the safe anchorage and freshwater stream, he establishes a settlement at Port Jackson—later named Sydney after the then British Home Secretary—near Botany Bay.

1793 The first independent settlers arrive to join the colony.

1797 John Macarthur, a lieutenant in the New South Wales Corps, introduces Spanish merino sheep, helping to lay the foundations of the future wool industry.

1798 A British expedition led by George Bass and Matthew Flinders circumnavigates Tasmania, showing it to be an island.

1801–1804 Matthew Flinders charts the mainland coast, establishing that the continent forms a single landmass. He recommends its name be changed from New Holland to Australia.

1804 Hobart in Tasmania is founded as a new penal colony.

1813 An expedition led by the journalist W. C. Wentworth pioneers a route across the Blue Mountains east of Sydney, opening up the continent's interior to settlement.

1817 Australia is officially adopted as the name of the continent.

1824 A penal settlement is founded at Brisbane.

1829 Perth in Western Australia is established by free settlers.

1835 Settlers establish themselves on the site of the future Melbourne, where a penal colony had previously failed to survive.

1836 Free settlers found the town of Adelaide.

1840 Transportation of convicts to New South Wales ends.

1842 Copper deposits are discovered and mined in South Australia *(below)*.

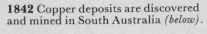

1850 The first Australian university is founded in Sydney.

1851 Gold is discovered, first at Bathurst in New South Wales, then in larger quantities at Ballarat and Bendigo in Victoria.

1854 The "battle" of Eureka Stockade—the only armed conflict to take place on Australian soil—pits miners against police and troops.

1855 The colonies of New South Wales, Victoria, South Australia and Tasmania are given self-government on local issues.

1859 Queensland is separated from New South Wales and given a similar constitution.

1860 Robert O'Hara Burke and William John Wills *(above)* complete the first overland crossing of the continent, but starve to death on the return journey.

1862 John McDouall Stuart makes the

54

first successful return crossing of the continent, from Adelaide to Darwin.

1868 Transportation of convicts to Australia finally ceases.

1872 Victoria becomes the first state to introduce free, compulsory, secular education.

1876 Truganini, the last Tasmanian Aboriginal, dies.

1880 Ned Kelly, the most famous of the bushrangers (outback brigands), is captured and executed.

1890 Western Australia is granted self-government on local matters.

1891 The Australian Labor Party is formed.

1901 On January 1, the Commonwealth of Australia is proclaimed in Sydney, federating the six separate colonies—now redesignated as "states"—into an Australian nation. The future King George V opens the federal parliament in Melbourne *(below)*. A restrictive immigration law, effectively preventing most Asians from entering Australia, heralds the "white Australia" policy.

1902 Australia extends political suffrage to women, becoming the second nation in the world to do so, after New Zealand.

1905 The Australian steel industry originates with the building of a blast furnace in New South Wales.

1909 Compulsory military training is introduced by act of parliament.

1914–18 World War I inflicts 226,000 Australian casualties, including 60,000 killed, from a force of some 400,000 men—all volunteers, because two referenda had rejected compulsory conscription.

1915 On April 25, the Australian and New Zealand Army Corps (ANZAC)

participate with great heroism in Allied landings at Gallipoli. Anzac Day *(monument, below)* is to become Australia's foremost day of national remembrance.

1919 The League of Nations gives Australia a mandate over the former German colony of New Guinea.

1927 The national capital is transferred to Canberra.

1928 The Flying Doctor service is established.

1939 With the declaration of World War II, Australia enters the conflict alongside Britain.

1942 Singapore falls to the Japanese and 15,000 Australians become prisoners of war. Japanese bombing raids severely damage Darwin.

1945 Australian forces participate in successful attacks on Borneo. The war ends with 30,000 Australians dead and 65,000 wounded.

1951 Australia, New Zealand and the United States join in the ANZUS Pact, promising mutual assistance in case of attack.

1954 Australia joins the South-East Asia Treaty Organization (SEATO).

1961 Oil is discovered in commercial quantities at Moonie in Queensland's Surat Basin, marking the start of the mineral boom of the following decade.

1962 The federal parliament gives adult Aboriginals the right to vote.

1965 An Australian military contingent (reaching 8,000 men by 1967) is sent to fight beside the U.S. Army in Vietnam.

1971 Australia brings back most of her troops from Vietnam, completing the withdrawal in 1972.

1973 Sydney Opera House *(below)* is completed.

1975 A constitutional crisis occurs in which Gough Whitlam, the first Labor Prime Minister in 23 years, is dismissed by the Governor-General Sir John Kerr.

1984 "Advance Australia Fair" replaces "God Save the Queen" as Australia's national anthem.

2

he discovered the great salt lake that now bears his name, but then marched, mostly alone, 1,500 kilometres along the southern Australian shore, on the coastal fringe of the barren Nullarbor Plain. He found nothing but sunbaked, waterless wilderness, setting a pattern of disappointment followed by most of his successors.

The population and economy of Australia were expanding at the same time as the country's known geography. New settlers were arriving there in floods. A total of 65,000 free immigrants landed between 1831 and 1840, at last outnumbering and eventually replacing the convicts. Many of the newcomers sought their fortune in the thriving wool trade, and export figures matched the population rise: from less than 80,000 kilograms in 1821 to more than 4,500,000 kilograms in 1840. For a time, the New South Wales government attempted to restrict any outward expansion, worried about the likely effects of uncontrolled development on the colony. Land grants ceased and a system of purchase took their place (the proceeds were used to subsidize emigration from Britain); in 1829, settlement outside the "nineteen counties" around Sydney was declared illegal.

No one paid much attention. If a man could not be a landholder, he would be a squatter, driving his herd of sheep—often bought on credit—into the virgin wilderness and establishing his "run". The word "squatter" had once been a term of abuse directed at vagrants; now, however, it was a way of life that attracted some of the colony's most venturesome spirits, and became a title borne with pride. In 1836, the government relented, granting official squatting licences for the interior.

Many squatters made huge fortunes (in time, the term "squattocracy" was coined to describe them), but their life was never easy. With a few unskilled shepherds, usually convicts, they used to set off for the middle of nowhere with their flocks of sheep and hope for a good increase. Drought, incompetence and sheer bad luck—not to mention the alarming fluctuations in the international wool market—caused many bankruptcies. As one squatter with a taste for wry verse wrote:

Of sheep I got a famous lot—
Some died of hunger, some of rot,

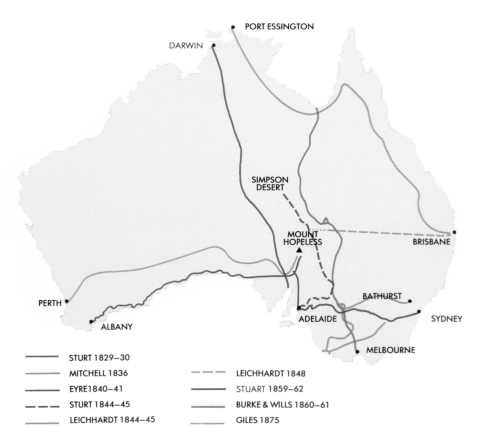

STURT 1829–30
MITCHELL 1836
EYRE 1840–41
STURT 1844–45
LEICHHARDT 1844–45
LEICHHARDT 1848
STUART 1859–62
BURKE & WILLS 1860–61
GILES 1875

The map *(left)* traces the routes taken by some of Australia's early explorers. One of the greatest was Charles Sturt, who in 1829 navigated the river system from Sydney to the south coast—an epic journey of over 1,400 kilometres. This success stirred his ambitions, and in 1844 large crowds

For the devil a drop of rain they got
In this flourishing land of Australia.

It was not an existence that appealed to everyone, and a majority of the new immigrants chose to remain in the towns. As early as 1850, 40 per cent of the total Australian population was concentrated in the six cities, especially Sydney. Indeed, after 1840, when the British government discontinued the convict transportation to New South Wales, the squatters were faced with an increasing labour shortage.

Colonial life was beginning to settle into a prosperous and regular pattern when suddenly Australia was thrown into the greatest—and also least expected—upheaval in its short history. In 1851, gold was discovered at Bath-

urst in New South Wales, and then a few months later at Ballarat, only 100 kilometres from Melbourne in the recently separated colony of Victoria.

The colonial establishment looked on the finds with horror. The *Sydney Morning Herald* predicted "calamities far more terrible than earthquakes or pestilence", while the *Bathurst Free Press*, closer to the scene of the action, declared that "a complete mental madness appears to have seized every member of the community". They had a point. Virtually overnight, Australian cities emptied in a fortune-hunting stampede, and, as word spread round the world, boatloads of eager new immigrants jammed Australian ports.

The people came from every social class. "There were merchants, cab-

men, magistrates and convicts," wrote one observer, "amateur gentlemen . . . fashionable hairdressers and tailors, cooks, coachmen and lawyers' clerks and their masters, doctors of physics and music, aldermen, an ADC on leave, scavengers, sailors, a real live lord on his travels—all levelled by community of pursuit and of costume."

The myth of the squatters was joined by the myth of the "diggers", as the prospectors came to be called—another comradely group, hard-bitten perhaps, but democratic to the core. Like all good myths, at heart it contained truth. Historians still argue over the extent to which the diggers transformed Australian society, most agreeing that they merely accelerated a process of growth that was already under

gathered at Adelaide (*above*) to watch him set off in search of an inland sea that he believed to lie at the heart of the continent. The sea proved to be a myth, however, and after months of trudging through scorched desert the party returned home, its leader's health broken and his dream shattered.

2

way. Certainly, the goldfields brought immense wealth to the colonies. At peak production, the Victoria fields yielded something like a third of the world's supply. Their most important contribution, though, was not to be measured in precious metal, but in the people who came to seek it. Successful or otherwise, most of them stayed on. In 10 years, the population of the country trebled, and it became obvious that Australia was no longer a colonial backwater to be administered from London for the convenience of the British government.

Even before the gold rush, Australians, especially the squatters, had agitated for representative government, and in the course of the 1840s had won a steadily increasing say in their own destiny. But the powers of the colonial legislative councils were restricted, and so was the right to vote. Given the huge rise in population, it was not a situation likely to promote stability.

In 1854, the gold miners—excluded, like most Australians, from the franchise—gave a warning of the sort of troubles that might be in store. Generally, the gold diggers were remarkably peaceable, and most observers agreed that in the Australian fields there was little of the general mayhem and murder associated with the California gold rush of 1849. But after three years' intensive panning, the easiest pickings had gone—and with them the good temper of those who had yet to make their fortunes. When the Governor of Victoria raised licence fees and enforced his decision with a brutal and incompetent constabulary, one group of miners took to arms. As an act of defiance, they fortified a hill at Eureka, near Ballarat, and demanded a list of reforms that included full manhood suffrage. The authorities, acting precipitately, used police and troops to storm the place: over 20 men died.

The incident was little more than a riot, provoked by genuine grievances and repressed violently by a panicky government. The trouble never spread, and there were no martyrs except the people killed in the fighting, who included policemen. Although the ringleaders were formally arraigned for high treason, all of them were acquitted. The miners' complaints—which mostly concerned the day-to-day administration of the goldfields—were soon rectified, and it seems likely that conditions would have improved even without the Eureka Stockade. As for manhood suffrage, when it was granted shortly afterwards only a minority of the diggers bothered to vote.

For nations, though, legends are often more important than facts, and symbols can carry far more power than dull reality. The image of those dusty, democratic diggers in that hot Ballarat summer, standing up for their rights against the oppressive might of the British Empire, has a permanent place in the Australian imagination. Mark Twain called it "the finest thing in Australian history", and references to the Stockade as the birthplace of Australian democracy are commonplace.

But perhaps the greatest significance of the episode is a negative one: it never happened again. Compared with other nations, old and new, the internal history of Australia is blessedly uneventful. The nation was built with sweat, not with blood.

By the end of the 1850s, five Australian colonies—New South Wales, Victoria, Tasmania, South Australia and the newly created Queensland—enjoyed responsible self-government on local issues, although London still controlled defence and foreign policy. Transportation was a thing of the past. The squatters might look back nostalgically to the cheap labour it had provided, but most other Australians were anxious to sell their own labour for the highest possible price and saw the convicts as unfair competition. In addition, they were an offence against their rising national pride. (There was one ironic exception: the colony in Western Australia, founded exclusively as a free settlement, was in such dire straits by the 1840s that its landowners successfully petitioned London for convicts. Despite loud criticism from the other colonies, transportation in the west continued until 1868; partly as a consequence, Western Australia did not achieve self-government until 1890).

If the colonies were becoming increasingly independent of Britain, they were even more independent of each other. The problems each faced were similar. The assemblies spent much of their time wrangling over systems of land allocation, and each colony suffered from the cycles of economic boom and bust that overlaid and sometimes masked their steady progress. But they faced their problems individually, adding tariff walls to the barriers of distance that already divided them.

Of course, variations in the continent's climate did impose some real differences between them. Queensland, for example, with its tropical northeast, devoted much effort to the cultivation of sugar cane. Plantations followed the pattern of the American South rather than the Australian, and to work them the sugar planters imported Polynesians—known as Kanakas, from the Hawaiian word for "man"—under

A 19th-century print shows troops and police storming the Eureka Stockade, near Ballarat, in Victoria, in 1854. Set up by angry gold diggers demanding lower licence fees and full manhood suffrage, the Stockade was captured after a short but bloody battle that left more than 20 men dead and 30 injured.

a bonded labour system that to the other colonies looked suspiciously like slavery. Faced with opposition from a clamorous labour movement in southern Queensland as well as from elsewhere, the northern planters attempted to secede. But the British government would have none of it, and the problem remained unresolved up to and beyond the turn of the century.

One factor common to Australians in all the nascent states was a growing fascination with the still unexplored interior of their own continent. Charles Sturt, one of the pioneers of inland voyaging, set off again in 1844, this time north from Adelaide, carrying a portable boat to sail upon the fabled inland sea. He got as far as the Simpson Desert before hunger, thirst and sickness drove his party back. A German immigrant, Ludwig Leichhardt, had better luck. Also in 1844, he set off on a year-long trek north-west from Brisbane; he discovered much good grazing land, before finally arriving at Port Essington, a short-lived settlement 180 kilometres east of present-day Darwin in the far north of the continent. But a second expedition showed him up as an incompetent organizer, and on his third, in 1848, he disappeared without trace in the central void—a tragedy that provided the 20th-century Australian novelist Patrick White with a theme for his epic *Voss*.

Exploration fever reached its climax in 1860, when the South Australian government offered a handsome cash reward for the first south–north crossing of the continent. Two very different expeditions strove for the prize. The first to reach the north coast was led by a hot-headed Irishman called Robert O'Hara Burke; but a combination of bad luck and bad judgement prevented Burke and his partner William John Wills from returning alive. The credit for achieving the first two-way crossing was to go to Burke's methodical rival, the Scotsman John McDouall Stuart, who made the return trip on his third attempt in 1862.

After Stuart's trip, even the wildest of optimists gave up hoping for their cherished inland sea, and no one was surprised when the heroic east–west

59

2

crossing of the continent by Ernest Giles in 1875 simply confirmed the bad news: Australia's heart was a scorched, stony waste. The vast Northern Territory would remain a useless desert. To the increasingly urbanized Australian population, living in the increasingly comfortable coastal cities, the bleak discoveries made little difference. But at least the explorers' tales found an eager audience. Few of the town-dwellers would ever see the outback, or "bush" as it was called, but for all of them it was becoming an essential part of their new Australian identity.

As if the wide-open spaces themselves were not enough, they gave the Australian folklore its most popular characters—the bushrangers. Originally, these had been escaped convicts and other desperadoes who had made a living by armed robbery on the fringes of the settled areas. In Tasmania at one time they had been a real menace. The gold rush had greatly expanded their opportunities and their numbers, to the extent that the mail coaches that served the diggings rarely travelled without armed escort. In the circumstances of the 1870s, the bushrangers took on a new role, that of Robin Hood, supposedly robbing the rich to help the poor. In actual fact, they robbed whomever they could, and there are no recorded instances of their acting as a welfare agency. But sensational reports of their exploits thrilled city people, and the rural poor were happy to see wealthy squatters suffer from the bushrangers' attacks. Bad roads and a much-hated police force were their greatest allies, and improved communications inevitably made the profession of bushranging obsolete.

Still, they had an undeniable appeal. When Ned Kelly, most celebrated of them all, was captured—in spite of a bizarre suit of armour he had fashioned to protect himself from police bullets—32,000 people signed a petition urging clemency. But the authorities hanged him anyway, in 1880; within a few years, the telegraph and the railway had made his legend as misty and far-off as that of Captain Phillip and the convict fleet.

The bushranger phenomenon was one symptom of the anti-authoritarian attitudes of the Australian people. Far more important was the steady rise of a powerful labour movement. It had had its origin in the nervousness Australian workers felt at the competition offered by convict labour, and it was quick to claim the Eureka Stockade as an early battle honour. Its first notable achievement, however, was the harrying of Chinese immigrants from the gold-fields and, by the time of the first inter-colonial trades union congress in 1879, one of its demands was for the establishment of a "White Australia" policy that, once implemented, only began to crumble a century later. Like the convicts before them, the Chinese were seen as a threat to the living standards of other Australian workers, and by the end of the 1850s most city-based Australians had high living standards to defend. In the following decades, they consolidated their position, with an eight-hour day agreed in most industries and wage levels that were the envy of the working-class world.

It was not, by European standards, a socialist movement. A strong Irish Catholic influence ensured a healthy respect for property and propriety as well as a dogged militancy; and most of the other elements to be found in Australia's powerful trade unions shared a genuine pride in being part of the immense and successful British Empire. Workers were far less interested in building a new kind of society than in carving themselves a healthy share of the society they already had. Only in the 1890s, when economic crisis shook every Australian colony and a campaign of nationwide strikes failed to keep wages up, did the labour movement go seriously into politics; but when it did, with the foundation of the Australian Labor Party in 1891, its candidates were soon being returned to state assemblies.

In time, they would be elected to more than state assemblies. The economic panics at the end of the 19th century finally pressured the six colonies into federation. The more perceptive politicians had been suggesting such a step for Australia for decades; and the imperial government in London, which had granted autonomy to a federal Canada as long ago as 1867, had no objections. Even so, negotiations—backed up by referendums in each state—took the best part of 10 years. Constitutions were drawn up, haggled over, scrapped, and drawn up again. Not until the first day of 1901 did the new Commonwealth of Australia come into existence.

The Constitution set up by the Commonwealth Act of 1901, as passed by the British Parliament, is still in force today. "The legislative power of the Commonwealth shall be vested in a Federal Parliament," runs Section I, "which shall consist of the Queen, the Senate and a House of Representatives." As the wording suggests, what follows is in essence a skilful amalgam of British and American usages.

The head of state is still the Queen—in her capacity as Queen of Australia,

The legendary outlaw and compulsive exhibitionist Ned Kelly fought his last battle with the police in 1880, wearing a suit of home-made armour *(below)*. A shot in the foot led to his capture. He was photographed *(left)* before he was hanged a few months later.

however, not as Queen of Britain—and the signature of her representative, the Governor-General, is required to validate legislation. He is bound, by the same conventions that exist in Britain, to accept the advice of "his" ministers; but he retains certain prerogatives, including the right—rarely used in practice—to dismiss governments.

The House of Representatives can be compared to the British House of Commons. Seats are distributed nationwide in proportion to population, and the House is responsible for initiating financial legislation. The prime minister and most of his cabinet are members, and elections take place at three-year intervals—although, like his British equivalent, the prime minister can call for a dissolution and a general election at any time during that period. The Australian Senate is much more like its Washington model than the British House of Lords. Twelve senators are elected from each state (plus two each from the two Territories), regardless of population, for a six-year term; half come up for re-election every three years. As a result, the balance of parties is rarely the same in the Senate and the House, and since the Senate has a veto as well as an amending power over legislation, the constitution discourages radical change.

Power is further shared with the legislative assemblies of each individual state, which retain considerable autonomy—although, since the Commonwealth was created in 1901, the federal government has tended to increase its authority at their expense. Generally speaking, the states are responsible for education, transport, law enforcement, health services and ag-

riculture; but since the federal government reserves itself unlimited powers to raise taxation, federal control of finance keeps state governments on a fairly tight leash. In addition to the various elected assemblies, the Constitution also provides for a system of Supreme Courts in each state, as well as a High Court of Australia, which handles both appeals from the states and strictly federal matters. Like the United States Supreme Court, the High Court can rule—and frequently has ruled—that legislation is unconstitutional and therefore void. The High Court is also

quite prepared to disallow laws extending federal powers into areas strictly of State concern.

The Constitution has been regarded, accurately, as a device for protecting "middle-class, property-owning conservatism"; but in franchise terms, it has always been robustly democratic. By 1901, indeed, Australia had as long a history of broad-based democracy as any nation in the world; even as early as 1860, the secret ballot practised in most Australian states was known to envious Britons as "the Australian ballot". The Franchise Act of 1902 extended federal

voting rights to all men and women over 21—except for the Aboriginals, who had to wait a further 60 years for the vote—and in 1925, perhaps fearful of the consequences of apathy, legislators made voting compulsory for all Australians. The Act was further amended in 1974, when the voting age was reduced to 18.

Independent or not, the new Commonwealth was firmly part of the British Empire. The late 19th century had seen a considerable amount of anti-British grumbling, especially among the Irish-descended community. After Federation, however, Australians seemed to settle down as the Empire's most loyal citizens. The "White Australia" policy was rigorously enforced—the Kanakas who had been brought to work in the Queensland sugar cane fields were nearly all sent home in 1906 and 1907. Its mechanism was a dictation test which any would-be immigrant had to take. Learning English was not enough to guarantee success, for the test could be conducted in any European language. English-speaking Chinese, for instance, often found themselves confronted with an examination in Italian. Whatever the rights or wrongs of the policy, it was effective: of a population just under 5 million in 1914, over 95 per cent were of British descent.

In any case, Australia's attachment to the British Empire was by no means entirely sentimental. The continent was practically defenceless: without the shield of Britain's Royal Navy, there was nothing—or so some alarmed Australians had been claiming for a generation—to guard it from the designs of rapacious European powers, not to mention the teeming Asian landmass just above the Equator. In return for

imperial protection, most Australians were content to pay their imperial dues—in loyalty, in financial contributions and, if the time came, in blood.

The outbreak of World War I took Australia by surprise, but the majority of its people supported Britain wholeheartedly and without any complaint. Although there was no direct threat to Australia itself, thousands of young men volunteered to fight for the Empire at the opposite end of the earth. The British, to begin with, were sceptical of the likely worth of what many senior officers regarded as raw colonials; but the test of battle proved that the Anzacs—the Australian and New Zealand Army Corps—were among the finest fighting soldiers of the war. Without conscription (vetoed by a nationwide referendum), Australia mustered more than 400,000 troops—11.2 per cent of the total population.

They were an unconventional army, easy-going and egalitarian, frequently insubordinate and rarely properly dressed. In action, though, they were a devastating force, and they had many admirers. Among them was the daughter of British Prime Minister Asquith, who wrote, "Their spirits and *élan vital* know no bounds and their physique and appearance are magnificent. Men like young gods, bare to the waist, burnt brown by the sun..." But the young gods were not immortal. More than half of them were to be wounded in the fighting, and some 60,000 never saw Australia again. They left their bones on almost every battlefield in France, in Palestine, in Syria and, above all, on the rocky little Turkish peninsula of Gallipoli.

It was at Gallipoli in 1915 that the Anzacs were blooded for the first time, in a daring invasion that was expected

to lead to the capture of Constantinople and the elimination of Turkey from the war. In fact, it was a disaster. Despite horrifying casualties, the invaders never succeeded in gaining more than a few kilometres of ground, and in the end the whole force was evacuated. Yet for Australians the heroism of the Anzacs transformed Gallipoli, their only wartime defeat, into a great moral victory. Their sacrifice was seen as conferring a new kind of mystic nationhood on the whole Australian people, their final coming-of-age. April 25, the anniversary of the landing, was celebrated as Australia's great national day, and even today, despite the passing of time and the debunking irreverence of Australia's young, it still carries great significance.

After the war, Australia sank into torpor, suffering badly from the slump that crippled the world economy in the 1930s. She was still very much under Britain's imperial wing—as late as 1939, for example, Australia's only full diplomatic representation overseas was in London; diplomatic relations with the United States were handled by an Australian counsellor attached to the British Embassy in Washington. In 1931, the British Parliament passed the Statute of Westminster, which conveyed unequivocal independence to the white Dominions of the Empire; far from being eagerly welcomed, the Statute was received by Australians with some suspicion, and they did not even ratify it until 1942.

World War II changed the old imperial relationship irrevocably. In some ways, indeed, the conflict could be described as Australia's involuntary war of independence, though few foresaw and even fewer would have desired such an outcome when the fighting

Families in Liverpool wait to board a ship to Australia in 1913. Lured by the prospect of regular work, high wages and generous subsidies from state governments, some 65,000 Britons annually emigrated to the continent in the years before World War I.

2

began. Unlike in 1914, Australia this time was in the front line. In World War I, convoys taking Anzac troops to Europe had been escorted by ships of the Imperial Japanese Navy, allied to Britain. In World War II, there was no such alliance: Britain's Far Eastern empire crumbled with terrifying speed before the onslaught of Japanese armies. Japanese troops invaded New Guinea. Japanese aircraft bombed Darwin. It was painfully clear that Britain, the bulk of her dwindling resources committed to a mortal battle in Europe against Nazi Germany, was no longer capable of affording the effortless imperial protection that Australians had taken for granted.

Under the pressure of events, the instinct for self-preservation proved far stronger than sentimental ties with the old Mother Country. If Britain could not protect her, Australia would have to look elsewhere. In an epoch-making speech at the end of 1941, Prime Minister John Curtin declared: "Without inhibitions of any kind, I make it quite clear that Australia looks to America, free of any pangs as to our traditional links or kinship with the United Kingdom." He added, "We know that Australia can go and Britain can still hold on." He did not say, but clearly he had it in mind, that events might turn out the other way around.

Of course, both Britain and Australia did hold on. After the grim year of 1942, the Pacific war settled down into a slow and usually bloody process of expelling the Japanese from the territory they had so quickly conquered. But the Australia that emerged in 1945 was not the Australia that had gone to war in 1939, and the world in which it found itself had changed even more profoundly. For one thing, the British

Empire had all but vanished, and although it took another 20 years for the ink to dry on the imperial death certificate, it was clear already that Australia's future security lay in her alliance with the United States.

More important still, the explosion of independent Asian nations from the ruins of the pre-war colonial empires vastly increased the complexity of the Pacific region, and presented Australia with her great post-war dilemma. Was she to remain an aloof, European outpost, or should she become an integral part of the new comity of developing nations? Was Australia's future to be one of apprehension or of enthusiasm—stagnation or opportunity?

It is only with the advantage of hindsight that 1945 appears as such a clear historical watershed. At the time, neither the changes nor the choices were immediately apparent to anyone, and the most general popular feeling was a profound desire to get "back to normal". By normalcy, though, no one meant a return to the economic doldrums and high unemployment of the backwater years of the 1930s; in any case, wartime developments—notably a vast increase in manufacturing in-industry, as the embattled nation had struggled to attain self-sufficiency—made such a prospect unlikely. People wanted peace and quiet—and, above all, prosperity.

After the first few unsettled post-war years, Australians seemed to find the answer to their prayers in the person of Robert—later Sir Robert—Menzies. As the head of a reformed but thoroughly conservative Liberal Party, he won electoral victory in 1949, and then remained Prime Minister—and, to all intents and purposes, the personifica-

tion of Australia both at home and abroad—for an astonishing 16 years. Menzies certainly delivered prosperity, and in terms of peace and quiet his government introduced little in the way of dramatic new legislation—too little, his detractors claimed. Yet paradoxically, this most conservative of politicians, who proudly announced himself to be the "Queen's man" and cherished the old imperial connection, presided over the most remarkable period of change in Australia's history.

The most startling, and perhaps the most permanent, alteration was in the composition of the Australian population. The old "White Australia" policy came to an end, at least in its British-only sense, and immigrants flowed in their thousands from continental Europe. It was reckoned that more newcomers came to settle in Australia during Menzies' term of office than during the half-century before World War I. They succeeded in injecting an element of cultural diversity and sheer vitality that many observers had found sadly lacking in the staid and somewhat provincial Australian society of the pre-war years.

In the post-war period, too, Australia began to discover for the first time the uncertain delights of a foreign policy at last independent of Great Britain. To some extent, it was simply a matter of confirming the change of mentors forced upon the nation by the war. The ANZUS Pact of 1951, a defence agreement between Australia, New Zealand and the U.S. that pointedly excluded Britain, was no more than a recognition of an altered balance of power. And Australians for the most part supported their new ally with the same loyalty they had previously given to Britain. Australian troops were the

BRAVE SERVICE ON BATTLEFIELDS ABROAD

An Australian despatch rider gallops past newly dug war graves at Gallipoli in 1915.

Fresh from campaigning in Syria, Australian forces parade through Beirut in 1941.

In 1966, Australian troops make their way past a bullock-drawn wagon in Vietnam.

On January 1, 1901, the Commonwealth of Australia was born. Instead of being divided into six British colonies, the continent was now a nation in its own right—but one that chose nonetheless to remain locked in the imperial embrace.

Compounded of both sentiment and self-interest, loyalty to the British Empire was to dominate Australian thinking for much of the next 50 years. It found dramatic expression during World War I, when thousands of men volunteered to fight for King and Empire.

Although lacking in parade-ground discipline, the Australians soon won a reputation for courage and endurance. Storming ashore on the Turkish peninsula of Gallipoli in 1915, they withstood a murderous enemy fire for eight months, suffering some 28,000 casualties before a withdrawal was ordered. By the end of the war, 330,000 Australians out of a population of less than 5 million had seen active service overseas; nearly 60,000 died.

With the outbreak of World War II, thousands more young Australians flocked to the far-off battlefields of Greece and the Middle East. This time, however, the conflict was to shatter rather than strengthen the old imperial ties. With the fall of Singapore in February 1942, Australians had to face the fact that they could no longer depend on British sea power for the defence of their homeland.

After the war they consequently sought to strengthen their ties with the one nation that could guarantee their security—the United States. A measure of the strength of the new relationship was the decision of the Australian government in 1965 to send troops to Vietnam. Once again, Australian forces—at one stage numbering 8,000 men—fought on foreign soil, but this time in response to developments on the Asian mainland to the north.

2

Wigged and gowned like their British
counterparts, two barristers hurry
along a hot Melbourne street on their
way to the law courts. Each state has
its own hierarchy of courts, whose
procedures and enactments are closely
modelled on England's legal system.

first to join the Americans in Korea in 1950; more controversially, Australia was just as quick to send fighting units into Vietnam in the 1960s.

The controversy took a little time to emerge, however. When Menzies left office in 1966, it seemed for a while that the Menzies era could continue without him. In fact, the Liberal Party stayed in power, following largely his policies, until 1972; and when the electorate chose to replace it with the Labor Party under Gough Whitlam, it was as much out of a sense of optimism for a new future as from a boiling discontent with the present. The late 1960s had seen vigorously expressed dissent at Australia's Vietnam policy, but the

protests never reached the nationally divisive proportions found in the United States itself; and in any event the last combat troops were withdrawn in 1971. But the 1970s, a decade that began with aspirations higher than ever before, proved to be a time of disappointment and uncertainty.

The Whitlam government began its term with a series of enthusiastic reforms that were largely welcomed—and, in many cases, long overdue. A national health service was organized, pensions and benefits were increased to the levels prevailing in most advanced countries, and significant amounts of money were at last spent upon the Aboriginal community. Whitlam also

relaxed restrictions on Asian immigration, as much to appease Australia's trading partners as to provide the country with immigrants. But the government soon began to run into economic difficulties, and it was not helped by the world oil crisis of 1973. Gradually its popularity decreased.

The manner of its going was unique in the history of the Australian constitution. The Senate—which Labor did not control—took the unprecedented step of blocking a money bill, thus effectively paralysing government; and the Governor-General, the Queen's representative in Australia, took the equally unprecedented—and to many Australians, much more shocking—

66

step of dismissing Prime Minister Whitlam, installing his Liberal opponent, Malcolm Fraser, at the head of a caretaker government, and calling an immediate election. Fraser won handsomely, but resentment at the action of the Governor-General was deep, and for the first time a significant number of voices could be heard calling for a republican constitution.

Fraser's government was soon almost as unpopular as its predecessor. The continued world recession was partly at fault, and Fraser's determination to reduce government expenditure and the role of government won him many electoral enemies.

Australians were also becoming aware of a new threat from South-East Asia—no longer military but economic. In 1970, Australia saw itself as the region's centre of high technology; by 1980, the colossal dynamism of Singapore, Taiwan and South Korea, not to mention the continuing development of Japan, was a challenge to its supremacy and left it with a growth rate well below that of its competitors. The neighbours were catching up.

As a result, Australians entered the 1980s much less sure of themselves than they had ever been before. Perhaps that was no bad thing: in the past, their self-assurance had often led to complacency and worse. When the Labor Party, under its new leader Bob Hawke, took power from Fraser in a surprise election victory in 1983, it was not a desire for socialism that inspired the electorate, but hope, the same hope for renewal that had brought in Whitlam 11 years before. And if Australians no longer thought themselves so favoured by fortune as they had a few years before, they still had a good deal to hope about.

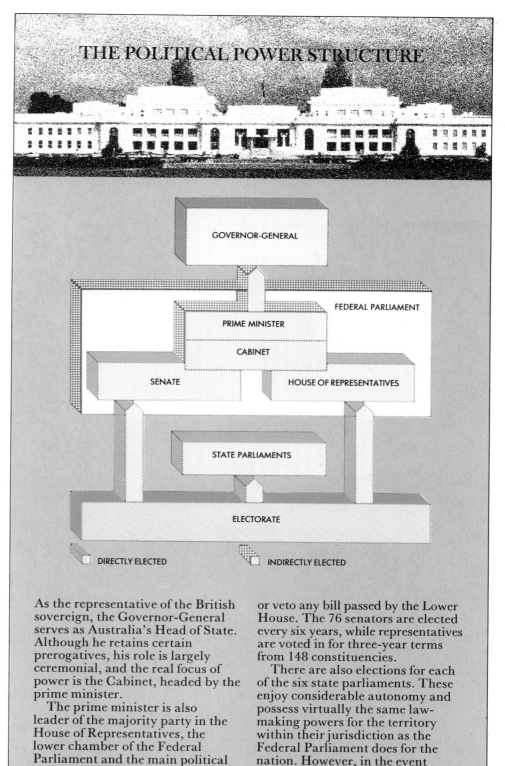

THE POLITICAL POWER STRUCTURE

GOVERNOR-GENERAL

FEDERAL PARLIAMENT

PRIME MINISTER

CABINET

SENATE

HOUSE OF REPRESENTATIVES

STATE PARLIAMENTS

ELECTORATE

□ DIRECTLY ELECTED   ▨ INDIRECTLY ELECTED

As the representative of the British sovereign, the Governor-General serves as Australia's Head of State. Although he retains certain prerogatives, his role is largely ceremonial, and the real focus of power is the Cabinet, headed by the prime minister.

The prime minister is also leader of the majority party in the House of Representatives, the lower chamber of the Federal Parliament and the main political battleground. The Senate, or Upper House, acts as a legislative watchdog, with the right to amend or veto any bill passed by the Lower House. The 76 senators are elected every six years, while representatives are voted in for three-year terms from 148 constituencies.

There are also elections for each of the six state parliaments. These enjoy considerable autonomy and possess virtually the same law-making powers for the territory within their jurisdiction as the Federal Parliament does for the nation. However, in the event of a conflict between state and federal laws, it is the federal laws that take precedence.

With candles to light their way underground, miners pose at the head of a shaft.

Smoke rises from the South Blocks Mine at the southern end of the lode.

EARLY DAYS AT BROKEN HILL

In 1883, tin was discovered at Broken Hill, a low, jagged ridge 200 kilometres from the nearest settlement in the New South Wales outback. The site subsequently also proved rich in silver, lead and zinc, but the settlers who flocked there faced harsh privations in the unforgiving semi-desert; drought, dust storms, scurvy, typhoid, lead poisoning from the mines and fatal accidents underground made their lives precarious and punishing.

Over the years, their community struggled towards stability. By 1910, when the first generation of children were young adults, steam trams ran in the main street and the more affluent families gave formal names to their corrugated iron dwellings. Sports and outings afforded some relief from the toil and hardship of their lives.

A newspaper, the *Barrier Miner*, reported their doings, from family picnics to the works' sometimes abrasive labour relations. The journal's photographer was Joseph Wooler, a millhand's son from Yorkshire. His photographs, some of which are reproduced here, give an eloquent picture of the rigours and rewards of life in an early Australian mining town.

A wedding group gathers outside the bride's home.

During a 1909 strike, workers converge on the company office.

Strollers pause in Argent Street, the town's main thoroughfare.

A galvanized iron veranda shelters a mother and daughter.

Spectators fill the town stadium for a football match.

A family picnics under gum trees in a creek outside the town.

A couple take a ride on one of the town's transport camels.

At Fremantle in Western Australia, jostling sheep stream on board a converted oil tanker for transfer to the Arabian Gulf, where they will be slaughtered according to Muslim ritual. Since 1970, Australia has become a major supplier of meat for the Middle Eastern market.

THE CURRENTS OF PROSPERITY

Australia is a land of visibly high living standards. Swimming pools glisten like sapphires in one out of every 10 suburban gardens; yachts skim across the harbours and bays; roads are crammed with cars, of which there are four for every 10 people, a rate of ownership second only to the United States. The endless stretch of suburban houses may seem monotonous to the beholder, but two thirds of them—a higher proportion than in most European countries—are owner-occupied. And going into one of those homes would confirm the impression that what ordinary Australians want, they can usually get. Colour television? Eight out of 10 homes owned a set within 18 months of their being put on the market in 1974. Refrigerators? Only 3 per cent of households are without one. And the purchase of these and other consumer items has not exhausted the average family's spending power; Australia has more savings accounts than people.

Nor do Australians have to work especially hard for their high standard of living. Effective trade unions, to which more than half the work force belong, have helped to give Australian workers some of the best conditions in the world. Having secured a 40-hour week for most workers by the early 1950s, they mounted a campaign for a 35-hour week in 1980, and have already achieved it in some industries. They have also secured annual leave entitlements of four—in many cases, five—weeks, plus a generous sprinkling of public holidays. Besides Christmas and Easter, Australians also have days off for agricultural shows, the birthday of the Queen and, in the case of Melburnians, for the Melbourne Cup, the nation's premier horse-racing event.

To help them enjoy their holidays, Australians get a 17.5 per cent bonus on their wages for the vacation period. Four out of five people can afford to spend the time travelling away from home. In addition to the popular activities of camping and caravanning, new diversions have been developed to cater mainly for the affluent middle class. An explosion of interest in skiing means that the winter resorts of the Australian Alps in the south-east are stretched to capacity. On any weekend, the wineries of Victoria's Murray Valley, South Australia's Barossa Valley, Western Australia's Swan Valley and the Hunter Valley, north of Sydney, are filled with visitors sampling the quality vintages. New summer resorts are mushrooming along the coasts of New South Wales and Queensland as an increasing number of people buy holiday and retirement homes.

The first-time visitor to the continent might agree that Australia is indeed The Lucky Country, as Donald Horne called it in the title of a best-selling book—a country where "Australians can live the life of the Mediterranean or the South Seas". However, another commentator, Craig McGregor, has

3

Carefully manipulated by a worker at Meekatharra gold mine in Western Australia, molten metal trickles from a crucible into an ingot mould. Meekatharra is one of several mining centres brought back into profitable production as world gold prices rose in the late 1970s and early 1980s.

detected a darker undertone to this hedonism: "It is almost as if Australians are out for a good time because they suspect it won't last."

His suspicions may be well founded, for in the early 1980s it seemed that Australia's spending spree might have temporarily come to an end. In 1982, the country had slipped to 15th position in the Organization for Economic Co-operation and Development's league of comparative living standards, having been placed fifth in 1955. In the same year, one out of 10 workers— mostly young people—were unemployed, and the annual rate of inflation stood at more than 10 per cent. Ominously, the nation's economic growth was being exceeded by the fast-emerging economies of the Pacific Basin— not only by Japan, whose own stunning post-war growth had stimulated much of Australia's development, but also by the newly industrializing countries such as South Korea, Thailand and Malaysia. Retail sales and construction starts were static. The Australian dollar was sliding against other currencies. Factory production was at a four-year low. And to cap it all, serious drought resulted in the poorest harvest for a decade, with some of the grain-producing regions experiencing their worst wheat yields since 1944.

For those Australians not too busy enjoying the pubs, clubs, barbecues and beaches, it seemed that the luck which many had come to see as their national birthright was deserting them. Bob Hawke, the Labor Prime Minister who took office in March 1983, thought so too. "There used to be some validity in the description of Australia as the lucky country," he told the nation. "But in the seventies the succession of fortuitous circumstances ceased. The

country should be brought to realize that it is no longer lucky. It has to do its own thinking and planning."

The fortuitous circumstances to which Hawke was referring stem from the fact that Australia is blessed with almost unlimited resources of food, minerals and energy, and in the past a minimum of effort and entrepreneurial skill converted them into the export and income that enabled Australia to buy the good life. Before World War II, Australia was a giant farm supporting itself by means of exports of wool and food to the industrialized nations of the West. At the time people used to say that the nation lived off the sheep's back, but from about 1960 onwards mineral resources came to challenge agriculture in importance. As luck would have it, the country was also a giant quarry. All it had to do to get rich, it seemed, was to

sell off chunks of the continent to the manufacturing nations, where pieces of Australia would miraculously be transformed into the consumer items that cram Australian homes. In referring to the need for Australia to do "its own thinking and planning", Hawke was drawing attention to the risks inherent in an economy over-reliant on primary products, many of them vulnerable to cyclical depressions in world trade at times of recession.

Old habits are hard to break, however, especially when they have been successful in the past. At the turn of the century, the export earnings generated by the sale of wool, wheat, meat and other agricultural produce helped to give the country one of the highest per capita incomes in the world; and by the beginning of World War II, the health of the economy was still dominated by a rural sector heavily dependent on over-

Chequering the sand of the desert like a giant board game, stacks of pipes lie on trestles at the Moomba natural gas field in South Australia's Cooper Basin. The gas is piped to Adelaide, Sydney, Canberra and elsewhere, mostly for use in electricity generators but also for domestic consumption.

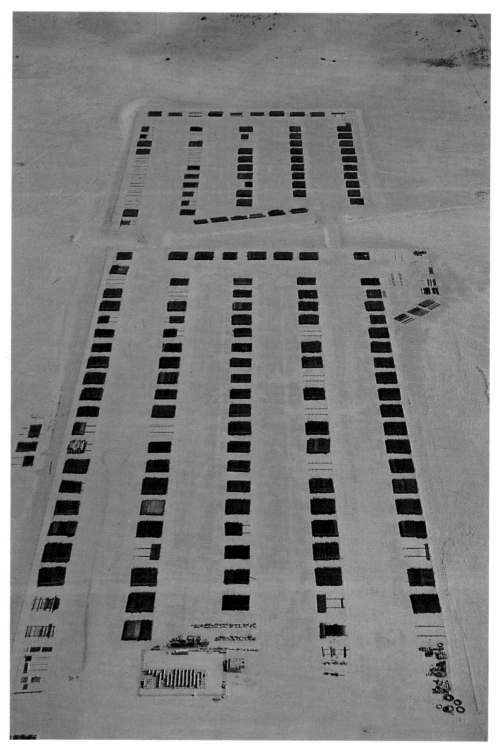

seas markets, especially Britain. In 1932, the Imperial Economic Conference in Ottawa led to an agreement which guaranteed an export market for Australian agricultural products in Britain, in return for preferential tariff treatment for British manufactured goods. The result, in 1937–38, was that almost half of Australia's imports came from the mother country, as did 55 per cent of its export earnings. Australia itself manufactured a small but growing proportion of its goods; the numbers employed in manufacturing climbed by over 50 per cent between the wars.

The war disrupted this pattern completely. Almost totally cut off from its major European customers and suppliers, Australia was forced to develop its domestic industry, including the manufacture of war-related products such as ships, munitions, aircraft and chemicals. The severing of the traditional trading ties also encouraged Australia to reorient trade away from Europe—a trend that was to gather momentum after 1945 in the burgeoning of commercial links with the U.S. and the countries of the Pacific Basin.

At the end of the war, Australia was committed to a programme of full employment. The post-war Labor government had more centralized power at the expense of the six states than any previous federal administration, and it drew up plans for major national development projects, designed partly to meet the possibility of unemployment in an anticipated post-war depression, and partly to show off the dynamism of the Australian economy.

The greatest single public works effort was the Snowy River Scheme. Established in 1949, the plan was to divert westwards and under a wild region of the Australian Alps part of the waters

AN UNEXPECTED GIFT OF THE SEA

At the Dampier salt project in Western Australia, harvesters and road trains dot the stark white of a salt field among the crystallizing ponds.

Sun and sea—two prime resources of Australia—combine to create the salt-making process. Over much of the country, the rate of evaporation far outweighs the meagre rainfall. Where these conditions occur over coasts with extensive tidal flats, it is possible to extract salt from sea water on a vast scale and at a low cost. Australia produces 6.7 million tonnes of salt a year, more than half of it at Western Australia's four salt fields, from Port Hedland in the far north to Shark Bay about 700 kilometres up the coast from Perth.

To make one tonne of salt takes some 60 tonnes of sea water—and a lot of time. The brine flows through a series of concentrating ponds, taking about 18 months to rise from a salt concentration of 2½ to 20 per cent. When the solids are ready to separate out, the brine is pumped into crystallizing ponds, where six months later a bed of white crystals forms. Mechanical harvesters move in to scoop the salt directly on to road trains at a rate of 1,000 tonnes an hour. Washed clean of impurities and unwanted minerals, the end product is drained for three months, then taken to Dampier for export.

Clean-washed salt pours from a conveyor on to a glittering stockpile to drain dry.

A road train is loaded with salt for export. Almost all of Western Australia's salt goes to Japan.

of the Snowy River, which hitherto had flooded tempestuously to the Victorian coast. The Snowy's waters were made to flow through tunnels blasted through the mountains into the Murrumbidgee and Murray Rivers, increasing fivefold the amount of water available for irrigation downstream in the fruit-growing and grazing districts of New South Wales and Victoria. And since the headwaters of the Snowy were about 1,000 metres higher than those of the Murray, the water dropping from one to the other was also used to generate electricity. Completed in 1974, the scheme now provides about 20 per cent of Australia's generating capacity, as well as irrigation for about 2,500 square kilometres of agricultural land.

Although the "Snowy" and other schemes were of incalculable value in fostering a national sense of achievement, they would have been white elephants if growth in the manufacturing sector had not been sustained—which meant attracting overseas investment. Before the war, over three quarters of Australia's national borrowing had been undertaken by federal and state governments and public authorities, with most of the money coming from London. But both the post-war Labor Government and its successor, the long-running Liberal–Country Party administration of Sir Robert Menzies, recognized the need for private capital from overseas. They had little difficulty in finding it. By the mid-1950s, about 70 per cent of the capital inflow came from private international investors, attracted by the nation's untapped riches, by her political stability, and by the pro-business attitude of the Menzies government.

The major source of this private sector investment was the United States.

A truck leaves the Jabiluka uranium mine in the Northern Territory, passing a geiger counter that checks its radiation level. Australia has about one fifth of the world's easily recoverable uranium reserves; most is sold under strict controls for generating electricity by nuclear reaction.

Canberra's closer political and defence links with Washington were mirrored by the growing importance of American business in Australia at the expense of British investment. American capital, for example, was responsible for the entire development and promotion of the Holden, which was manufactured in Sydney and marketed as Australia's "own car". Even though the British Motor Corporation also began vehicle manufacture in Australia in the 1950s, the battle for the driver's seat was won decisively in the end by American interests. General Motors (the manufacturers of the Holden) and Ford virtually monopolized the booming market in large, six-cylinder family saloons and station wagons.

Growth in the manufacturing sector was also accelerated by the imposition of import restrictions in 1952—a step taken to protect the nation's foreign exchange reserves. The metal trades, also cushioned by high customs duties on goods of foreign origin, grew so fast that by the 1960s they were employing almost 50 per cent of the manufacturing work force. The cities were alive with the throb of heavy industry. New enterprises began. Aluminium was transmuted in the metallic alembics of the electric furnaces; steel and tin-plate mills began to roll. Oil, chemicals and shipbuilding—all were on a rising curve, and a sense of fresh possibility for Australia was in the air.

None of this growth could have been achieved had there not been more workers than ever before to keep the wheels of production turning. At the end of the war the population of Australia stood at little more than 7 million, and it was not highly qualified in educational terms. Only 25 per cent of the teenagers had attended secondary

school in 1938; as a result, the country was sadly lacking the skills needed in the new industries. "Populate or perish" became a national slogan, which reflected both the need to increase the labour force and a sense of insecurity at a time when the nationalist and communist movements in South-East Asia were signalling the end of direct European influence in the area. Because the British Isles, the traditional source of immigration, failed to satisfy the need, the Labor government was obliged to look elsewhere, and particularly to displaced persons from the Baltic states and central Europe. Immigrants came flooding in from Greece, Yugoslavia, Holland, Italy, West Germany, the United States and Scandinavia. Almost three quarters of the one million increase in the work force between 1941 and 1961 were "migrants", as Australians call immigrants who have come to

stay. Greece alone supplied so many that Melbourne, the new home city for most, soon housed the third largest Greek community in the world.

Some of the migrants took rural jobs—like the Spanish farm workers who became Queensland sugar cane cutters, or the Italian smallholders who set up market gardens on the outskirts of the cities. But most went into manufacturing, working alongside the native Australians and British migrants in the expanding factories and workshops. Some of these migrants became captains of post-war Australian industry: Sir Peter Abeles, an Hungarian refugee who started work as a truck driver, built up and became chairman of the international travel conglomerate TNT; Sir Tristan Antico, an Italian, founded Pioneer Concrete Services; and Sir Arvi Parbo, the Estonian-born chairman of Western Mining Corpora-

tion, saw his firm's activities help spark
the mining boom of the late sixties.

The British immigrants continued to
dominate the influx, however, partly as
a result of travel subsidies designed to
boost their numbers. In return for a
commitment to work in Australia for a
specified period, they were paid back
the cost of their journey less 10 pounds
sterling—a scheme that earned them
the nickname of "ten pound poms".
One of the most successful of the new
Australians, and certainly the most
flamboyant, has been Alan Bond, who
arrived in Perth in 1950 with his family,
because his father, who was in poor
health, had decided to leave his native
London for warmer climes. At the age
of 15, two years after arriving in
Australia, Bond left school and became
an apprentice signwriter for a minimal
weekly wage; but by the time he was 19
he had formed a painting, decorating
and repair company, taking "jobs no
one else would do", he recalls.

House painting was only a beginning, and he soon moved into one of the
traditional Australian business activities—property speculation. For his
first big deal he borrowed a substantial
sum to buy land on the outskirts of
Perth: "I built bitumen roads there and
sub-divided the land and sold it cheap-
ly. After four months I had paid back
the bank, and the rest was profit."
Bond was off and rolling, buying land
and then sub-dividing it into residen-
tial 1,000-square-metre blocks in a succession of shrewd, if often risky deals.
In the mid-1960s, one of his boldest
gambles was to develop a tract of sand
dunes 60 kilometres north of Perth as a
yachting centre and holiday resort
called Yanchep Sun City. His aim was
not only to make money, but also to
create a base from which he could

mount a challenge for yachting's most
prestigious trophy, the America's Cup,
which had been held by the New York
Yacht Club for more than a century.

Bond's first challenge failed, and
worse was to come. The property boom
that had fuelled his ambition collapsed
in 1974, and seemed set to return his
business career to square one. But he
survived, and even managed to sell Sun
City to Japanese buyers in order to
fund his next venture: investment in
Australia's booming energy developments. Again, he was in the right place
at the right time. In 1978 he bought a
stake in the Cooper Basin, a semi-
desert region on the South Australia–
Queensland border that was already
supplying natural gas by pipeline to
Adelaide and Sydney. In the year of his
acquisition, however, substantial oil
reserves were also discovered. The find
boosted Bond's capital dramatically.

It helped him to finance the acquisition
of Western Australia's only brewery,
the Swan, and also procured him a slice
of a diamond mine in the north-west
corner of the state.

With his second fortune he renewed
his quest for the elusive America's Cup.
Although another attempt in 1980 had
ended in failure, on September 26,
1983, his larger-than-life story became
part of Australian sporting mythology.
Tied 3-3 with its rival after six races, his
yacht *Australia II* surged ahead of the
American boat *Liberty* in the decisive
seventh race to take the most jealously
guarded trophy in sporting history. A
quest that had cost Bond a sizeable fortune over a period of 10 years had
finally ended in triumph, and the celebrations that kept millions of Australians up all that night were for him a
personal fulfilment.

When Alan Bond arrived in Australia,
the rural sector was still providing almost 90 per cent of the export earnings.
More than half that total came from
wool, with wheat, dairy products, meat
and sugar making up the balance. Australia, it was estimated, owned roughly
one sixth of the global sheep flock, from
which it produced about a quarter of
the world's wool clip.

Not surprisingly, then, the mainstay
of country life was, as it continues to be,
sheep farming, and its most respected
citizens and the graziers—landholders
with large holdings dating back in
many cases to the days of the original
"squattocracy". By their prosperity
and the scope of their social life, incor-
porating balls, polo matches, European travel and visits to the cities to see
friends and attend agricultural shows,
these native aristocrats distinguished
themselves from smaller-scale farmers.

THE SUBTERRANEAN LIFE OF THE OPAL MINERS

A tourist bus stands among the spoil heaps that lie by each mineshaft in the opal fields. Visitors may sift through the heaps for stray stones.

A sign warns of the danger of disused mineshafts in the town.

Miners in a rocky gallery work with pick and shovel.

Opals were discovered in 1915 at Coober Pedy, an isolated spot in the centre of South Australia, hundreds of kilometres from the nearest town. The town now houses 4,000 or so inhabitants and is still the main opal-producing centre in Australia—or anywhere else. Ninety per cent of the world's opals come from Coober Pedy or from nearby Andamooka.

In spite of continuous mining since 1916, it is estimated that less than 2 per cent of existing opal stocks have been brought to the surface. Mining operations are kept to a small scale by government policy. The law permits each miner to stake only one claim of 50 square metres, and no more than four people may join their claims into a partnership. Large mining concerns therefore have no place in the town, which remains a rough and ready community of individuals hoping to make a fortune by their own efforts.

To gain their chance of wealth, the miners have to contend with a multitude of discomforts, of which the worst is extreme heat. For four months of the year, the average temperature is 36°C, rising to 40°C or more for days at a time. Dust from the mining operations often swirls into blinding storms that make landing and taking off at the town's rocky airstrip a nerve-racking business. The only water in the town comes from a saline borehole, and fresh water, provided by a solar desalination still, is precious: each resident is allowed 450 litres a week.

To escape the crushing heat, many people at Coober Pedy have retreated underground, into caves dug out of the slope where the opals were first discovered. The gypsum in the rocks makes it possible to hollow out sizeable chambers that will not collapse. Some homes are quite spacious and even luxurious; and if the occupants decide to add an extra room by hollowing out the rock, there is always the chance that they may discover a few gems.

Miners with friends and family relax in one of the comfortable, neat underground houses.

A priest celebrates a wedding in the grotto-like Anglican church opened in 1977.

3

Yet the latter too lived comfortably for the most part, in wide-verandaed homes screened for protection against the omnipresent bush flies.

A portrait of a typical small sheepman, then or now, would probably show a stocky figure with a frank and open countenance and a deeply tanned complexion. He would be dressed in elastic-sided boots, moleskin trousers, a check shirt and would be wearing, with self-consciousness betokening un-familiarity, a plain tie. But the give-away of his country origins would be a wide-brimmed hat, worn with pride perhaps bordering on ostentation. "The bigger the brim, the smaller the property," an ironic wisecrack warns.

The currency of such farmers' lives are sheep's fleeces, and removing these has always been the main business of the station year. Freelance shearers, paid by the number of animals they clip, are hired for this work. Today, with the use of trail bikes for rounding up the sheep flocks and aircraft for keeping track of them, farm work has become increasingly mechanized and staffs have been shrinking; but in the post-war years, a number of resident hands were also needed to occupy themselves with such tasks on the station as fencing, servicing the windmills and pumps to assure the water supply in artesian areas, protecting lambs from dingoes and other predators, and rounding up the sheep with the aid of kelpies and other sheepdogs.

The cattle stations—the other props of the pastoral economy—were even less labour-intensive. Most of them were usually unfenced, and might consist of little more than a central homestead around which the animals would roam at will within a radius of 15 kilometres or so, whose limits were defined only by the need to return to the local watering-home to relieve thirst.

Unsurprisingly, Australian agriculture in general, and the pastoralists in particular, were often accused of being unscientific and a trifle lackadaisical in their approach. Competition—in the case of wool, from synthetic fibres—and the threat to the farmers' traditional main market as Britain negotiated for EEC membership, forced a change of attitude. In an effort to remain competitive, Australian farmers used more machinery, adopted scientific breeding methods and increased the average size of their holdings—measures that reduced the rural labour force to about one in 20 by the 1960s. The ability to adapt to new conditions was well illustrated by the wool industry, which had earned as much as a third of Australian overseas sales in the pre-war years, but it had been hit hard by the loss of markets during the war and by a severe drought in the mid-forties. Thanks to better breeding techniques, pasture improvement and the introduction of the myxomatosis virus to control the plague of rabbits that had been ravaging the grazing land, wool output began to rise again at the beginning of the 1950s. The resurgence came in time for the farmers to cash in on a new demand for woollen garments generated by the presence of thousands of American troops in Asia because of the Korean War. In five years, fleece prices rocketed tenfold.

By 1952, though, the pent-up spending power that was unleashed by these windfall earnings had produced the first of the post-war inflationary waves. When the boom burst, the credit squeeze that brought inflation to heel left wool growers with well-stocked pastures financed at high interest rates, but with dramatically reduced returns with which to pay off the loans. Faced with low prices and the contraction of the Yorkshire woollen mills that had provided the main market since the early days of settlement, many wool growers switched to wheat and cattle production, or sold out and joined the drift back to the cities.

But some graziers elected to ride out the trough, just as their fathers had in

In a Queensland banana grove, dogs greet a worker bringing in a load of fruit. Pineapples, pawpaws and mangoes are also grown in Australia's tropical and sub-tropical regions, and the temperate areas produce apples, pears, plums and berries.

the Depression. Their optimism was justified. Although wool prices did not return to the levels of the early 1950s, the industry regained prosperity with new markets in the rapidly growing Japanese mills. In the 1970s they were joined by the fast-emerging woollen industries of South Korea and Taiwan. By the middle of the 1980s, in spite of desperate drought at the start of the decade, Australia was still the world's dominant wool exporter, producing almost a quarter of the global clip.

The pattern of finding new markets was repeated across a wide range of rural exports. Australian cattlemen, for example, climbed aboard the American fast-food bandwagon by producing the low-grade beef for making hamburgers. By the 1970s, the U.S. was Australia's biggest customer for beef. And the drive for new markets knew no political barriers, as the wheat board proved when it made significant grain sales to the People's Republic of China at a time when the Canberra government did not recognize the Communist administration in Peking.

By the 1980s, the farm sector was contributing 6 to 7 per cent of national output, and though this figure was well below the 20 per cent of 1900, a third of Australia's export earnings were made by rural products. Wool was being challenged by wheat as the chief farm export. The nation was still the second largest sugar exporter in the non-communist world, with overseas sales to the value of over A$700 million in 1982. And beef, buoyed up by its new American markets, sold steadily, to the value of over A$1,000 million in 1982.

And yet the post-war achievements of Australia's farmers have been eclipsed in the popular imagination by the suc-

3

cesses of the mining industry, which caused one of the wildest stockmarket stampedes seen this century. Almost every generation in Australia since the middle of the 19th century has caught the gambling fever produced by a major mineral discovery, but no one was prepared for the mineral boom of the 1960s. Australia entered the decade as a country that banned iron ore exports, had virtually no nickel production, and needed to import all but a trickle of its oil. Yet 10 years later it was one of the world's leading iron ore and nickel ex-

porters, and it had lifted its crude oil output from 5,000 to 65 million barrels a year. During the sixties, bauxite production increased twelvefold, manganese production multiplied 13 times, tin output quadrupled, the tonnage of black coal doubled and copper and lead output improved by 50 per cent.

Discoveries were made in all parts of Australia. On the island of Groote Eylandt in the Gulf of Carpentaria, massive deposits of manganese were found in 1966. In the same year, Australia's largest company, Broken Hill

Proprietary (BHP), in partnership with the world's biggest petroleum company, Esso, struck oil and gas in the Bass Straits. The field, between the Victoria coast and Tasmania, was to become the mainstay of the nation's supplies. The sixties also saw the development of the Weipa bauxite reserves in the York Peninsula, which had been unearthed a few years before, and the opening of the huge Blackwater coal mine in central Queensland.

Perhaps the most spectacular discovery of the decade was made in the

86

In Tasmania's mountainous south-western corner—one of the world's last temperate wildernesses—the concrete of the Gordon dam retains 12,000 million tonnes of glassy-smooth water. The dam was completed in 1974 to help keep pace with the island's projected demand for electricity.

Pilbara region of Western Australia where in 1938, for strategic reasons, the federal government had stopped the development of iron ore reserves. The ban remained in effect for 15 years after the war, because of a gloomy warning made by the official government geologist in 1938 "that if known supplies of high grade ore are not conserved, Australia will become an importer rather than a producer of ore".

One man who knew that this view was wrong was Lang Hancock, a pastoralist in the Pilbara. In November 1952, he and his wife had been flying across the Hamersley Range when a storm forced their plane below cloud level. Hancock noticed a metallic sheen in the 60-metre-high cliffs of the gorge in which he was flying. It indicated that they might be rich in iron, and when he returned later to verify this, he found that he was not mistaken. Since the embargo was still in force, Hancock kept the secret to himself, but when the ban was lifted in 1960, he took executives of the British mining house Rio Tinto Zinc to the area, where geologists traced bands running for hundreds of kilometres across the ranges. Asked to estimate the amount of reserves in the region, an American steel executive replied that it was like trying to "calculate how much air there was"; workers boasted that one mountain was so rich in iron ore that it rusted in the rain.

The discoveries could not have been better timed, since world iron and steel output expanded dramatically in the 1960s. Japan, in particular, developed an insatiable demand for ore to feed its steel industry, which quadrupled output between 1960 and 1970. Australia had to call on foreign capital to develop the Pilbara, and companies such as Kaiser, AMAX and Mitsui

A WORLD CENTRE OF PEARLING

The ketch-rigged pearling luggers that operate out of Broome, more than 2,000 kilometres north of Perth in Western Australia, have not changed much since they were first used in the 1880s, but the pearling industry—one of Australia's oldest—has been through many vicissitudes. Even before the luggers arrived, divers were collecting high-quality pearl-shells from the tropical waters offshore. By 1910, Broome was the world's biggest pearling centre, with up to 400 craft crewed by Japanese, Malays, Filipinos, Chinese and others. They faced great hardships, from cyclones to the decompression sickness known as "the bends", to bring home the shell that supplied the world's demand for mother-of-pearl.

Broome's prosperity declined in subsequent decades, partly as a result of two world wars, partly because plastics began to erode the market for mother-of-pearl. But after World War II, new techniques for culturing pearls revived the fortunes of the community. By the early 1980s there were five thriving pearl-culture farms in the town's vicinity, and pearl and pearl-shell production were a multimillion dollar industry.

The luggers' pearling trips to the oyster beds 6 kilometres off the coast are normally limited by tidal conditions to 10 days' duration. The pearler's year is divided into three seasons. Between April and August, young shell is separated from the large pearl-shells and kept alive on board ship in 3-metre tanks of circulating sea water; on the farms it is seeded to produce cultured pearls. From September to December, only large pearl-shells are collected; they provide mother-of-pearl for the manufacture of knife-handles, buttons, furniture inlays and similar articles. The wet season—December to March—means a rest for the diving crews, and the luggers are laid up on the beach.

Two pearling luggers sail out to the oyster beds. Each can bring back as many as 6,000 young oysters.

In a sorting shed on land, a mountain of large shells is sorted and graded.

Oysters drying in the sun festoon the rigging of a lugger, while the crew sort and pack the shells.

The Catholic church at Beagle Bay, 130 kilometres north of Broome, shimmers with pearl-shell.

joined the Australian companies CSR and BHP to invest hundreds of millions of dollars. The money was spent on building ports such as Dampier and Port Hedland, establishing new towns in the Western Australia outback, and laying railway tracks for thousands of kilometres across the desert.

On April 4, 1966, as the development of the Pilbara region was getting under way, attention was diverted by the announcement of another discovery some 960 kilometres to the south near the historic mining town of Kalgoorlie, the scene of the gold rushes of the 1890s. This time the mineral involved was nickel, which 17th-century metallurgists called "devil's copper" because of its misleading resemblance to that much-sought metal. It set the fuse for the biggest Australian sharemarket explosion of the century.

The timing of the strike was crucial. The American aerospace and defence industries involved in the Vietnam War and the space race, had a boundless appetite for nickel at a time when the world's major producer, Canada, was having supply problems. To capitalize on this demand, Western Mining Corporation, which had made the discovery, developed the nickel mine with unprecedented speed; within a year of the announcement of the strike, ore was being produced, and by August 1967 the first shipments of nickel concentrate had been dispatched. But while Western Mining made the discovery, the company which rocked the international investment world in the nickel boom was Poseidon—a symbol of the get-rich-quick fever gripping Australia. In 1969, Poseidon shares stood at 80 cents; in April 1970, after its miners had made a nickel discovery at Windara in Western Australia, its shares had soared to A$286. And yet all the company possessed at the time was a row of drill holes, a line of trenches and some rough mining camps in the bush.

Nickel hysteria swept Australia, with Poseidon tipped to go to A$500 a share. Rumours of fresh strikes sent waves of prospectors to stake mining claims in the most unlikely areas. New companies having only the most tenuous connections with mineral exploration were floated almost daily on the stock exchange. Many joined the boom by changing their names: Glacarium, which owned an ice rink in Sydney, became Nickel Development; Project Development, which built houses and sold meat, became Project Mining. Ordinary people who had never bought a share in their lives began punting on a dizzy assortment of facts, half-truths and bare-faced lies. Dubious practice was rife. Shares in one mining company rose from A$3 to A$96 in three days, after its chairman told a reporter that his nickel prospects could be bigger than Poseidon's. The share prices subsequently collapsed, and a report found that the prospect consisted of "a few panned samples and a hazy identification of some excavated rock".

It was not only Australia that was infected by the nickel bug. The rest of the world joined in, quadrupling overseas investment on the Australian stockmarket between 1966 and 1971. These funds, known because of their short-term duration in the country as "hot money", combined with hundreds of millions directly invested in long-term projects, pushed foreign capital inflow to torrential levels, fuelling fears that Australia had sacrificed its economic independence for the fast buck.

With newspapers filled with stories of share traders making thousands of dollars a day, most Australians must have felt they were on the verge of the greatest era of prosperity in their history. Few heeded what the bush poet Banjo Paterson wrote at the turn of the century: "I saw bank booms, land booms, silver booms, Northern Territory booms, and they all had one thing in common—they always burst."

And so it happened with the minerals boom. With so much of the Australian mining industry mortgaged to the needs of the Western industrialized nations, it took only a fall in demand to prick the bubble. That came in 1971, when the Nixon administration, faced with soaring trade deficits, imposed a surchange on imports. Japan, America's major trading partner, was thereby forced to cut back on exports and thus reduced its demand for raw materials, of which Australia was a major supplier. In 1972, Japanese steel mills reneged on contracts to take 100 million tonnes of Australian iron ore. In 1974, when the U.S. dollar crisis had eased and signs of economic recovery were under way, the oil crisis intervened, once again cutting manufacturing output in the industrialized nations and reducing their imports of raw materials.

For Australia, the resultant problems were compounded by factors that weakened the nation's ability to compete in world markets. At the start of the 1970s, when unemployment stood at only 2 per cent, the unions had the whip hand and were quick to use it. The number of strikes rose sharply as unions confronted the labour-starved employers with wage claims. In 1971, earnings rose by 13 per cent compared with an annual average for the previous decade of 5 per cent. Inevitably, wage rises were reflected in raised prices, and inflation, which had averaged 2.5 per

In a warehouse at Kwinana, a port 32 kilometres south of Perth, a team of government inspectors sample the lower slopes of a mountainous store of wheat awaiting export, to ensure that it is free of insects. Australia is the world's third largest exporter of wheat, surpassed only by the U.S. and Canada.

3

cent in the 1960s, rose to 6 per cent in 1971 and 8 per cent in 1972.

The difficulties of limiting wage settlements to a level acceptable for the economy as a whole were exacerbated by the system of Australian industrial relations. The work force is highly unionized, but split between more than 300 unions, operating within a legally established system of arbitration and conciliation commissions at federal and state levels. Although the Australian Council of Trade Unions tries to coordinate its members, it has little power to control them. Membership of a union allows an Australian to gain not only a national wage increase (given to all workers, unionized or not), and an industry award based on comparisons with other sectors and skills, but also an "over-award" wage rise negotiated with the individual employer.

With the unions exercising the considerable leverage they command, wages

rocketed by 29 per cent in 1974 and 15 per cent in 1975, and prices rose by 15 per cent and 13 per cent in the same years. Business, struggling with accelerating costs and double-digit interest rates, reduced investment by 5 per cent, plunging the country further into recession. The economy, which had been growing by 7 per cent per year at the start of the decade, became virtually stagnant. The gloom in industry was summed up by a car sticker of the time: "Will the last businessman to leave Australia please turn out the lights."

After more than a decade of virtually full employment, the number of people out of work more than doubled in 1974. Job losses were particularly severe in the textile, footwear and clothing industries, which had been hit hard by tariff cuts introduced by the 1972 Labor government. Redundancies were also heavy in the vehicle industry, with layoffs at Ford, Chrysler and General Motors Holden, and the closure of British Leyland's plant in Sydney.

The number of jobless continued to rise after the coming to power, in 1975, of Malcolm Fraser's Liberal–Country Party, which had vowed to give precedence to the fight against inflation. But despite tight budgetary and monetary policies, inflation did not return to single figures until 1978; and even then, price rises of 8 to 9 per cent made Australian goods uncompetitive in the international marketplace. As so often in the past, when economic salvation came in 1979–80, it came not so much from Australian economic policies as from events outside—this time, another oil crisis in the Middle East.

Australia was in a better position to weather the new oil crisis than most countries, thanks to the development of the Bass Strait fields, which ensured that at least 70 per cent of the country's needs could be met from its own resources. In addition, a string of discoveries and developments in the 1970s had reconfirmed Australia's position as a major exporter of energy. The huge open-cut coal mines of central Queensland were expanding output; oil and gas finds in the Cooper Basin were substantial enough to justify the construction of a huge liquid-petroleum gas production plant; and the discovery of massive deposits at Roxby Downs had quadrupled the nation's uranium reserves. Coal, which in the early 1970s accounted for less than 5 per cent of Australia's overseas income, became the country's most important commodity, comprising 14 per cent of export sales in 1983 and making Australia one of the top three exporters in the world.

As world energy prices continued to rise, many foreign countries decided to

At the little town of Woy Woy, a retirement haven and holiday resort 80 kilometres north of Sydney on the coast of New South Wales, children dig happily for crabs on the beach. Despite the economic fluctuations of recent years, most Australians can still enjoy a carefree life rich in outdoor leisure.

harness the continent's resources by locating energy-intensive industries, such as aluminium production, down under. At a time of world shortage of aluminium, Australia stood to reap huge benefits, but the rush to capitalize on the opportunity led to an unseemly squabble between state governments, with each state, irrespective of its energy capabilities, vying to offer the aluminium companies electricity prices at bargain basement level. In the space of two years, plans for the building or expansion of aluminium smelters were announced for Portland in Victoria, Gladstone in Queensland, and Tomago, Lochinvar and Kurri Kurri in New South Wales' Hunter Valley, and an alumina smelter was completed at Wagerup in Western Australia.

But by 1982, the world was in recession again, reducing both the need for energy and resources. Once again the prophecy of Banjo Paterson had been fulfilled. When aluminium prices fell, the Portland smelter was shelved, the Lochinvar project was cancelled and the Kurri Kurri expansion was halted. In the same year, the Japanese announced that they were having second thoughts about taking liquid petroleum gas from the Cooper Basin; they also cut coal imports from Australia, and announced to Australian steel producers that they were substantially reducing their orders. The boom that had lifted the Australian economy in the early 1980s to a growth rate twice that of most major Western countries had fizzled out almost before it had begun.

Unemployment, which had dipped slightly in 1980 and 1981, climbed to a new post-war high, with one in 10 workers—some 600,000 people—out of work. Particularly depressing was the fact that one in five teenagers was jobless, and the average wait for a first job after leaving school had risen to 10 months. The jobless were cushioned to some extent by dole payments, but life on these was far from easy. In 1984 unemployment benefits for a single person aged 18 or more with dependants amounted to 89 Australian dollars a week, and for a married man with dependants to A$149, compared to an average national wage of A$300.

Of course Australia was not the only country to feel the effects of recession in the 1980s, nor could all the blame for its economic misfortunes be laid on external factors. The boom of 1981 had recalled some of the worst aspects of the late 1960s, particularly in industrial relations. When workers in other industries saw the high wages being paid in the resource sector, the unions decided to press for increases beyond those recommended by the federal and state wage tribunals. The result was the worst outbreak of industrial disputes for 10 years, with employees in almost every sector resorting to strike action. During one especially bad period, Sydney had no electricity, trains, rubbish collection and telephones—prompting the exasperated newspaper headline, "Is anyone out there working?"

One of the most worrying aspects of the unbridled wage demands was that they reduced Australia's competitive position against the fast-emerging economies of the Pacific Basin. In the 10 years to 1983, Australia's average annual growth was 2.6 per cent, compared with 3.7 per cent in Japan and over 7 per cent in Taiwan, South Korea, Hong Kong, Singapore, Malaysia and Thailand. Forecasts suggest that the gap between Australia and its neighbours will close further, with Asian economies expected to grow by between 7 and 9 per cent in the 1980s, while Australia maintains its pace of the 1970s. It was the need to place the economy on a more competitive basis that prompted Labor Prime Minister Bob Hawke—a former trade union leader—to call a national summit meeting of business and union leaders shortly after he took office in 1983.

After four days of debate, an accord was hammered out. The union leaders agreed to postpone indefinitely any new salary demands in exchange for price controls and a vast public-works programme aimed at creating jobs in Australia's sagging construction industry and other areas of the economy. The government also tried to make Australian industry more competitive internationally by opening the market to imported goods, hoping that Australian manufacturers, in order to survive, would start to produce technologically advanced manufactures for the expanding economies of its neighbours.

In the wake of the conference, Australia stood at an economic crossroads. The choice was for the country to remain little more than a continent-wide quarry, letting other industrialized nations turn its massive resources into goods, or to use the skills of its work force and businessmen to become a major manufacturing power. Were it to succeed in the latter course, its economy could become one of the most dynamic in the region. Some years ago an American journalist described Australia as the Disneyland of the Pacific: "The size and scale of its resources development task made it Frontierland, Adventureland and Tomorrowland rolled into one. But there is a touch of Fantasyland about it too—will the development really take place, or is much of it wishful thinking?"

THE WEATHER'S UGLY MOOD

From time to time the usually equable Australian climate turns cruelly capricious, causing damage on a grand scale. Normally, the continent is influenced by a mass of warm, moist air, centred over Indonesia to the north-east, which ensures some rainfall over most of the country. But once every five years or so, a ridge of high pressure dominates the region, and that can mean no rain at all.

The phenomenon of recurring changes in weather pattern, known to meteorologists as the Southern Oscillation and as yet unexplained, presages the coming of droughts that can turn the land to dust, killing off crops and livestock and facing farmers with ruin. A further hazard of the dry spells are bush fires, which in bad years claim a harrowing share of forest and farmland.

But the end of a drought can bring its own dangers. Barometer readings can then drop unusually low, torrential rains follow, and enormous areas of topsoil, desiccated in the preceding months, are swept away by floods.

A bather runs for shelter as a dust storm sweeps across Port Phillip Bay towards Melbourne on February 8, 1983. Carried by winds from the drought-stricken outback, the storm raged over the city for 40 minutes, blinding motorists and littering the streets with 11,000 tonnes of topsoil.

Stirred by the spiralling updrafts of wind known as "willy willies", a haze of red dust hangs over the town of Pooncarie, in New South Wales.

Guarded by a lone fence, South Australian pastureland scorched by the sun stretches to a dusty horizon *(right)*. When drought hits the land, it is usually the sheep and cattle farmers who head the economic casualty list. As soil deteriorates and pastures are over-grazed, many farmers sell their poorer-quality stock for rock-bottom prices and carry feed to the rest *(above)*. But if the drought is prolonged, the feed may run out. Then the choice is moving the animals to cripplingly expensive grazing areas or shooting them. Either way, years of work can be cancelled out in a few months.

Bush fires sweep through tinder-dry
forest in Victoria after a prolonged
drought *(left)*. Such conflagrations are
a regular feature of life in the
outback, and each community has its
own force of volunteer fire-fighters,
equipped with water pumps, walkie-
talkies and knapsack sprays *(above)*.

FLOOD: THE ORDEAL AFTER THE RAINS

A truck noses its way through rain-
flooded bushland on Western
Australia's Kimberley Plateau. The
downpours that often follow a long
spell of dry weather can inundate
vast tracts of territory, disrupting
transport and communications
and briefly turning the land into a
huge reservoir.

4

With his dogs to help him, a grazier herds a flock of Merinos by motorcycle in the Riverina district of New South Wales. The dry grassland plains fringing the outback provide pasture for millions of sheep, which outnumber the human population of Australia by almost 10 to one.

THE MYSTIQUE OF THE OUTBACK

Behind the inhabited coastal fringes of Australia lie more than 7 million square kilometres of arid plains, marginal pastureland, deserts, scrub, salt lakes and worn-down mountain ranges that together make up the outback. The region has no formally defined boundaries—not, that is, unless you count the 10,000 kilometres of 2-metre-high fence built to keep dingoes out of the Queensland and South Australia sheep country. It begins where the population density falls to a level that can be measured in square kilometres per person rather than people per square kilometre; and in Australia that means about four fifths of the land area—almost the whole of the country west of the 5,000-kilometre Great Dividing Range, across which 19th-century explorers travelled in search of the vast inland sea they were sure lay at the heart of the continent.

But the explorers were geological ages too late. One hundred and fifty million years ago, during the Jurassic era, giant plesiosaurs with ranks of teeth in a 3-metre-long head hunted where now only salt-pans shimmer in the sun; and 25,000 years ago, 2-tonne, plant-eating marsupials browsed on lush vegetation, which has now been replaced by sand dunes and stony gibber plains. Today, the bones of these creatures lie entombed under the salt crusts of lakes that may fill with water only once in a lifetime. There is rain in the Australian outback, but it is sporadic and can cause as much damage by flooding as the severe droughts that went before it and that will invariably follow. A child born in one of the isolated settlements in the dry centre of the continent might not see rain until he is more than five years old.

Unsurprisingly, in view of the prevailing aridity, the principal colour of the outback is brown. On its fringes, the land is khaki-toned and liberally sprinkled with the grey-green of water-conserving mulga and mallee shrubs. Scattered through its width are small townships—dusty settlements that often consist of a street of one-storey buildings, many built out of corrugated iron. Between the towns there are only isolated homesteads, linked to one another and to civilization by lonely roads that are lined, perhaps, by a single telephone wire. The homesteads survive because part of the outback receives just enough rain to serve as pasture; others draw water from some of the thousands of artesian bores drilled into the huge underground reservoirs of the Great Artesian Basin, which underlies the outback's eastern section.

Much of the outback is genuine desert—or, to be more exact, many deserts, each with its own individual character. North of Lake Eyre and straddling the state line of South Australia and Queensland is the Simpson Desert, a fiery gridiron of longitudinal dunes covering an area of 140,000 square kilometres. Here, in 1845, the

explorer Captain Charles Sturt and his party were marooned by drought for six months, surviving in an underground shelter as the temperature outside climbed to 70°C. With them they had a boat which they had dragged hundreds of kilometres to sail on the fabled inland sea. West of the Simpson, the fiery red sand dunes give way to the thorny Great Victoria and Gibson Deserts, the latter named after an explorer who died of thirst there in 1873. In turn, these deserts pass into the Great Sandy on Australia's north-west coast. In this region, the inhabitants of Marble Bar have to endure a mean December temperature of 33.8°C, and once experienced 160 consecutive days when the shade temperature rose at least four degrees above that figure.

All these deserts surround the geographical heart of the continent. Here the colour of the land deepens to tawny ochre, then to a sunburned red. This is the Red Centre, so called because of the iron oxide in the rocks, which turns them the colour of rust. Worn flat by millennia of erosion, the Centre survives immutable and immemorial, caught in a Sleeping Beauty trance from which only some great geological convulsion could awaken it. And at the midpoint of the Centre itself is Ayers Rock—a smooth sandstone monolith rising 348 metres from a flat plain—that is one of the great natural wonders of the world.

Human works are few and far between in the outback, for such a hostile land cannot support a large population and probably never will. Western Australia, a quarter of the size of Europe, has just over 1.25 million inhabitants, and most of them live in Perth and the other coastal towns. The Northern Territory, covering 1.3 million square kilometres, is home to only one tenth of

that number, the majority in Darwin and Alice Springs. Outside the small townships, the outback population is scattered on sheep and cattle stations that may be as large as Belgium.

Roads are the main means of communication—long, unbroken stretches of dirt track with signs warning the driver that it is 300 kilometres to the nearest available water. But the aeroplane too is an everyday lifeline, ferrying supplies to the dispersed oases of human habitation. QANTAS, Australia's international airline, started life in the outback as a tiny, one-plane service between remote bush settlements; the initials stand for Queensland and Northern Territory Air Service.

Although the sprawling red outback, with its thin sprinkling of settlements, seems far removed from the bustling cities on the coastal fringe, the interior and its people remain an ever-present force in Australian affairs. The outback

lurks like some evil djinn trapped in an insecurely corked vessel, and from time to time drought sets the djinn free, reminding the coast dwellers how narrow their foothold in the country is. When the inland pastures have been seared by months of drought and the sheep and cattle have to be slaughtered and buried in mass graves, a cold draught can be felt in Australia's financial institutions, and the Sydney shopper faced with rising food prices receives a jolting reminder that the nation lives closer to the land than its population distribution would suggest. Since Federation, most of the large swings in the fortunes of Australia's political parties have followed serious droughts.

Just how disastrous the absence of rain can be was brought home to Australians in 1983, the year that saw the climax of the prolonged drought they christened the Big Dry. All through January the country withered as strong

winds whipped up the parched soil in the outback and carried it to the cities of the south and east, blinding motorists and clogging machinery. But worse was to come. On February 16—Ash Wednesday—gale-force winds drove bush fires along 750 kilometres of coast from Adelaide to Melbourne. In some places, the fires caused a vacuum into which fireballs were sucked at speeds of more than 160 kilometres per hour. After two days, seven townships had been wiped out, some 2,000 homes had been destroyed and more than 70 people had lost their lives.

For most of the nation's farmers, the Big Dry lasted for two years. Faced with diminished reserves of fodder and badly grazed pastureland, many sheep farmers had to cull their flocks and sell off all but their best ewes at rock-bottom prices. Some owners received only 5 dollars for animals that would normally have sold for 20 to 30 dollars a head. They were the lucky ones: one New South Wales farmer was forced to sell 180 of his ewes at 10 cents each. In parts of the Northern Territory, the drought—though less severe—ran on for a further six months, and when rains finally came they caused the worst flooding in 10 years.

Much of that torrential downpour was caused by a cyclone—another familiar weather hazard in the outback. The most disastrous of the great winds of recent years was the one that struck the city of Darwin on Christmas Day in 1974. Weather-satellite pictures had shown a large mass of cloud in the Arafura Sea between Australia and New Guinea as early as December 21, and these clouds had taken on the ominous circular form that was typical of a developing typhoon. For the next three days the storm intensified, but its slow and steady course south-westwards suggested that it would pass harmlessly north of the Australian coast, 100 kilometres or so out to sea.

In the morning of December 24,

however, Cyclone Tracy, as it was named, suddenly changed course to the south-east on a direct line for the city. Weather officers who had been following its progress immediately notified the local federal authorities, who decreed that half-hourly cyclone warning messages should be transmitted on the local radio and television channels. But in the festive atmosphere of Christmas Eve, few people paid much attention to the broadcasts. Attempts to call a meeting of the local Emergency Committee failed, because most of the members proved to be inextricably enmeshed in the office-party circuit, and amazingly nobody even thought to forewarn federal government officials in Canberra. The result was that the city was almost entirely unprepared when the cyclone struck in the early hours of Christmas Day.

The exact force of the wind is not known, because the Darwin Airport anemometer broke when registering a speed of 275 kilometres per hour. Its blast lifted roofs and cars, and demolished whole storeys of houses. When it abated some four hours later, 67 people were dead, and 90 per cent of the buildings in the city had been devastated. Since Cyclone Tracy, Darwin has been rebuilt—for the third time, as the city had been flattened by a cyclone in 1897, then by Japanese bombs in 1942. It has been estimated that a cyclone can be expected to pass within 100 kilometres of Darwin once every six years, so the permanence of the latest settlement cannot be taken for granted, despite all the precautionary measures to render the new structures windproof.

Natural disasters like droughts and cyclones are tangible evidence of Australia's harsh nature, but to newcomers to Australia it is not just the outback's objective dangers that threaten. It is the land itself, its emptiness, its lack of definition, its unyielding primitivism, the bizarre character of its flora and fauna. A new generation of Australians, however, has come to appreciate the country's awesome beauty—the red monoliths of the Centre, the rare water holes cold and clear and deep, the primordial splendour of the vast, patterned landscapes laid out under a cerulean sky. For these people, the emptiness of the bush is its greatest asset, providing a refuge from the crowded and polluted cities, and a source of spiritual renewal for those suffering from overexposure to the multiplying stimuli of modern life.

Tragically, the true heirs of the Outback, the Aboriginals, have been dispossessed of their inheritance, stripped of their culture and forced into a marginal existence on the fringes of white society, all in the space of less than 200 years. When the first white settlers disembarked at Botany Bay in 1788, there were probably 300,000 Aboriginals in Australia and Tasmania, including the deserts of the outback. Between them, they spoke more than 500 different languages grouped into about 30 related language families, although one such family—the Pama–Nyungan—was used by over about 80 per cent of the continent's population.

The Aboriginals used to be semi-nomadic hunter-gatherers in their traditional lifestyle, ranging over limited stretches of territory in their search for food and water. Vegetable food was the main element in the diet of the desert tribesmen, but meat was available for those who had learnt to understand the bush's rhythms. Insects were commonly eaten. The wichety grub—the larval

The sun's first rays light up verandas lining the main street of Coolgardie, in Western Australia's goldfields region. Like many boom towns of the 1890s' gold rush, Coolgardie declined when the seams ran dry. Now with a resident population of only about 700, tourism is its main resource.

stage of a moth—was considered a delicacy, while honey ants and various species of bee supplied a source of sugar. Apart from lizards, larger animals were not everyday food items. The men did most of the hunting. They speared kangaroos, emus, possums and snakes, and the large lizards called goannas, trapped and caught other animals, and speared or trapped fish. Coastal Aboriginals knew the places where whales stranded themselves. Most smaller food items—seeds, yams, roots, honey, fruits and berries—were collected by the women. The Aboriginals devoted much time and energy to the important task of locating water; they relied on memory and good navigation to find the water holes and soaks whose location they were taught from early childhood.

To catch large prey, the Aboriginals used a number of ingenious weapons, including the woomera, or throwing-stick, which could hurl a spear more than 100 metres, and the various kinds of boomerang, which were effective up to a distance of about 50 metres. The well-known returning boomerang was used mainly for games and for diverting prey into traps or ambushes. The women's essential tool was the coolo-mon—a curved dish, usually hollowed from a knot of wood, used for carrying water, digging for termites and other food, and pounding the seeds used to make their cake-like bread. Apart from these items, they had few material possessions; and those they did have were portable, so that they could move quickly and take advantage of the seasonal changes. At night they slept out in the open air or in shelters made from the local vegetation. To keep warm, they lit fires by using friction sticks, or they simply curled up with each other

4

AN ANCIENT AND SACRED MONOLITH

or with the semi-domesticated dogs—cousins of the dingo, which arrived on the continent with visiting seamen from the Asian mainland about 4,000 years ago.

Since the food resources of the outback are limited, the Aboriginals did most of their hunting and gathering in one or more nuclear family units; but they owed their allegiance to tribes, formed by the splitting-off of related groups after an increase in population and the inevitable establishment of new territories. An individual's social obligations were dictated largely by observance of extremely sophisticated and complex kinship systems. Children were often betrothed at birth—and frequently, in the case of girls, to partners much older than themselves. Those who received a wife were generally obliged to make repayment at the time of the marriage or at some time in the future—usually in the form of an exchange of sisters. Although many men had only one wife at a time, the ramifications of the kinship system meant that men and women had available a number of potential partners, who provided them with an accepted channel for pre-marital or extra-marital liaisons. Actual polygamy was sometimes practised, with some men having as many as 30 wives, the later ones often pressed on to the husband by the first wives, because they wished to reduce the burden of food-gathering.

Despite the rigours of their harsh environment, the Aboriginals had a well-developed social life and a sense of aesthetics. They held ritual gatherings attended only by men, but they also staged non-sacred ceremonies for both sexes, called corroborees, for leisure and relaxation. These were sometimes attended by as many as a thousand

A rail assists climbers on the Rock's western face, the usual point of ascent for visitors.

Ayers Rock glows a rich orange in the light of the rising sun. In the background rises Mount Olga, 32 kilometres to the west.

In the continent's dry centre, Ayers Rock—known to the Aboriginals as Uluru—rises almost sheer from a featureless plain dotted with spinifex grass. Three kilometres long and almost 9 kilometres in circumference, this vast sandstone monolith shows, iceberg-like, only a small part of its bulk. Though this portion reaches 348 metres, the rock outcrop of which it is part extends much further underground—at least 2,100 metres.

The Rock is geologically unique. The largest formation of its kind in the world, it is 600 million years old. Soil cannot cling to its rounded back, whose bare stone surface alters colour dramatically with the changing light of day. Yet in its hidden crannies the Rock shelters water holes with a rich animal and plant life, and make it a vital landmark on Aboriginal trails.

Tiny figures descending the Rock reveal the massive scale of one pitted sandstone flank.

4

A road sign on the Stuart Highway, the main north–south route linking Darwin to Adelaide through the centre of the continent, warns motorists to watch for unwary wombats. Slow-moving and shy, these burrowing marsupials are frequent casualties when crossing roads at night.

tribal members, who came together for dancing and singing, some of the songs being elaborate chants containing several hundred verses that built up complex word pictures through symbolic allusion and imagery. There was also a wide repertoire of songs concerned with everyday events. The rhythm of the songs was marked by beating together boomerangs, clubs or skin pads; in the north, additional instrumental accompaniment was provided by the didgeridoo, a drone trumpet fashioned from a hollow sapling or from a section of bamboo with the inner nodes taken out. On informal occasions, an undecorated didgeridoo up to 2 metres long was used, but for ceremonial purposes the natives chose an instrument about 5 metres long and profusely ornamented with designs and feathers.

Different tribes had their own distinctive styles of art, including carved totems, body decoration and paintings on either bark or stone. For paints, they used such natural pigments as yellow or red ochre, pipe clay or charcoal, mixed with water or the juice of an orchid that acted as a fixative. The paints were applied with a stick, a finger or a feather brush, and often augmented with bird down or hairs that were collected from certain plants. Most of the Aboriginal paintings had a religious significance, and the artists—always men—either executed traditional designs or created new ones from visions they had seen in dreams. Some works had a sinister significance. If an Aboriginal wished an enemy dead, he commissioned an artist-magician to send the intended victim a death message— usually a simple dot-and-line design burnt on to a stick.

At the core of the Aboriginals' world picture was a belief in the "Dream-

time", a period when supernatural beings moved over the earth and gave it form and life. The Dreamtime was also a parallel reality in the present, for they further believed that all men were the descendants of these mythical ancestors and were irrevocably linked to them and the land they had created. Every feature of an Aboriginal's tribal territory—each tree, rock and water hole—contained the spirit of his or her ancestors. Individuals not only knew their way about their land, but also knew its legendary history and its spiritual inhabitants; and because they believed that they were identical with their ancestors, they could feel the land was their own creation, and a journey through it was to experience not only the comforting presence of the past but also the joy of regeneration.

But the Dreamtime became a nightmare when the white settlers arrived. From the beginning, there were clashes

between the Aboriginals and the newcomers. At the time of the dispatch of the First Fleet, the British government had provided high-minded guidelines for the treatment of the King's new stone-age subjects, and the dutiful Captain Phillip had tried to follow them as best he could. To begin with, he attempted to protect the native population from depredations, even ordering the public flogging of a convict who had stolen some fishing equipment from an Aboriginal tribe. But attempts at an enlightened policy foundered in the great gulf of incomprehension that yawned between two utterly different societies; the flogging episode, for instance, was greeted by shock and outrage from the tribespeople whom it was supposed to appease. After a while, maddened by thefts—an entirely meaningless concept to the Aboriginals—Phillip was reduced to launching a punitive expedition against them—a concept just as meaningless, and murderous to boot.

Thus the pattern of communication was established. The Aboriginals were regarded as a nuisance, to be driven off into the emptiness with whatever force was needed for the purpose. Not only did they have to make way for the well-armed Europeans, but for their sheep and cattle too. As settlements proliferated on Australia's coasts and began to expand inland, the continent's original inhabitants were faced with disaster. Casual killings were commonplace and usually went unpunished. The Aboriginals retaliated, and demonstrated their skill in guerrilla warfare; but they were outgunned by superior technology and could not put up a sustained resistance. In all Australia's history, probably less than a thousand Europeans were killed by Aboriginals, while at least 10 times as many tribesmen died at the hands of the European.

The fate of the Tasmanian Aboriginals was the worst of all. Their women and children were often given to the convicts, their men were butchered for sport. In 1804, the year of the first white settlement at Hobart, there may have been as many as 7,000 of them. In 1824, there were only a few hundred left. In 1831, a somewhat shamefaced government exiled the surviving 190 Aboriginals to an island reservation where, surrounded by the consolations of the Christian religion, they obligingly died out; the last full-blood succumbed in 1876. It is not an episode remembered in Australia with pride.

On the mainland, too, Aboriginals were rounded up into missions and reserves, where alcoholism joined illness in drastically reducing their numbers; many died of European diseases, lacking immunity to smallpox or even to common complaints such as measles. Set up mainly between 1900 and 1930, the reserves purportedly offered the Aboriginals "protection"—in reality, a euphemism for segregation. In the state of New South Wales, for example, until 1939, anyone of apparently Aboriginal blood could be forced to live on a reserve under white supervision, and black children were not allowed to attend white schools—which meant that very few Aboriginals received any schooling at all.

In fact the Aboriginals were very much a non-people as far as white Australians were concerned. They were not counted in the census; they were not allowed to vote; they were forbidden to own land; they had to have official permission before they could accept a job, and their wages were paid to the local "protector" of Aboriginals—usually a policeman. Those who lived on the reserves were required to do 32 hours' unpaid work each week; defaulters earned themselves a summary punishment of up to two weeks in jail. Insubordination or other offences could result in an Aboriginal being sent away to a prison island for an indefinite period of time. Although the officials would never openly admit it, the unspoken assumption that underlay such severe treatment was that the mainland peoples, like their cousins in Tasmania, would quietly die out. As late as 1939, the Australian Modern Reference Encyclopaedia confidently proclaimed: "The Aborigines, of many tribes, of primitive habits, and a low order of intelligence, are disappearing."

The encyclopaedia was wrong. From about the time of World War II, their lot began steadily to improve. First, their numbers, long declining, began again to increase. Despite a disturbing rate of infant mortality and short life-expectancy, the high birth rates and increasing access to medical services meant that the Aboriginal population started to grow and even to outpace that of the white Australians. In 1971, the first year that the Aboriginals were included in the census, there were estimated to be about 140,000 in the country. By 1976, this figure had been revised upwards to 160,000; and in the 1980s, a Human Rights report gave the population level as upwards of 200,000. By the end of the present century, it is estimated that the number will have reached approximately 300,000—a significant figure, as it will mean that the population will have returned to the level it had reached before the white man arrived in 1788.

Once it became apparent that the Aboriginals were not dying out, the policy of confining them to reserves was changed in order to bring them into the economic and social life of the Australian community as a whole. The word "assimilation" was widely adopted, and in 1951 it was the official strategy of the federal government. The implications of this policy were spelt out at a conference of the Commonwealth and State ministers concerned with Aboriginal affairs in 1964: "The policy of assimilation means that all Aborigines and part-Aborigines will attain the same manner of living as other Australians and live as members of a single Australian community enjoying the same rights and privileges, accepting the same responsibilities, observing the same customs and influenced by the same beliefs, hopes and loyalties as other Australians."

This was progress, and the policy of assimilation coincided during the first half of the 1960s with the disappearance of discriminatory laws. Commonwealth legislation that had previously restricted Aboriginal access to social security benefits was amended in 1960, and the electoral rules were changed in 1962 so that the adult Aboriginals got the vote. In 1967, the government held a referendum to find out if the Australian population wanted the Aboriginals to be counted in the census, and if they wanted the federal government to make laws for the Aboriginals rather than the state governments, as had previously been the case. By a margin of 10 to one, the yes vote won.

However, by this time, critics of the government's policy were complaining that the assimilation programme was simply a cover for the destruction of the Aboriginal's traditional way of life. Instead, they demanded that the government set up a policy of integration,

4

which would protect Aboriginal rights while also leaving them free to follow their own traditions if they chose. The Aboriginals themselves, inspired by the example of minorities in the United States and New Zealand, had started taking militant action to further their aims. The campaign came to focus on land rights.

The first important test case came in 1968, when a group of clans from the Gove Peninsula in the Northern Territory decided to contest the granting of a special mineral lease to a mining company, who intended to quarry bauxite on their territory. Before the case came to court, the Prime Minister of the day made it clear that their demands would not be acceded to. But when the judge in the case ruled that the Aboriginals held no proprietorial rights to land, even though they had lived on it for generations, the public protest that followed ensured that a change in land rights law became a major issue in the 1972 election.

The incoming administration appointed a High Court judge to advise on how best the Aboriginals' land rights could be established. His recommendations that those living on government reserves should be given non-transferable freehold title and that others should be able to make claims on the basis of tradition to any unalienated Crown land were finally passed into law by the succeeding Liberal government of Malcolm Fraser. The Aboriginal Land Rights Act undoubtedly proved the most significant advance in their status in two centuries. By 1983, 28 per cent of the Northern Territory had been given back to them on freehold title, while a further 19 per cent was under claim; and in South Australia and Western Australia also, substantial tracts of outback land had been returned to their original owners.

It was the wool trade that originally drove the European settlers into the bush and towards confrontation with the Aboriginals. For more than a century, the nation lived off the sheep's back, with wool providing the nation's main export commodity. Today sheep-farming is still big business, although cattle-raising now presents a challenge in terms of the economic activity generated. The grazing territories of the two put together cover some 475 million hectares—more than four times the total area occupied by all the other Australian land-use systems combined. Of this total, sheep stations account for 170 million hectares, and are chiefly situated on the south-east and south-west inland plains, where the rainfall averages about 27 centimetres a year. Cattle stations take up the remaining hectares, mainly in northern and central Australia, where the land is too arid for sheep to survive.

Perhaps due to their long pedigree, the owners of the large sheep stations have always occupied a special niche in Australian society, constituting almost a native aristocracy. As early as the middle of the 19th century, travellers were observing their resemblance to the land-owning families of Britain. A Scot called John Hood, who visited Australia in 1841 to see his squatter son, described such a station: "I have passed a most delightful day at Camden; a more agreeable English-looking place I have not seen. The house, the park, the water, the garden, the style of everything and of every person, master and servants, resembled so much what one meets with in the old country, that I could scarcely believe myself sixteen thousand miles from it." Thirty years later, the English novelist Anthony Trollope, after he had travelled to a lush, well-watered area of the Victoria bush, described ironically how the social status and manners of the Australians were defined by head of sheep: "The number of sheep at these stations will generally indicate with fair accuracy the mode of life at the head stations: 100,000 sheep and upwards require a professed man cook and a butler to look after them; 40,000 sheep cannot be shorn without a piano; 20,000 is the lowest number that renders napkins at dinner imperative; 10,000 require absolute plenty, meat in plenty, tea in plenty, brandy and water and colonial wine in plenty, but do not expect champagne, sherry or made dishes. . . ."

Today, the large wool-growers continue to enjoy a fortunate lifestyle, which is closely modelled on that of the landed gentry back in England. Their children are usually educated at private boarding schools. At social events, the young men are distinguishable from their counterparts at county shows in England only by the wide-brimmed felt hats that they wear with their sports coats and cavalry-twill trousers. All of this is in marked contrast to the rough and ready image presented by the small sheep farmers, and by the men who perform all of the manual work on the stations—the shearers, shed-hands and roustabouts.

Despite great advances in scientific breeding, the control of diseases and the improvement of pastures, life on Australia's sheep stations has not changed much since the time of the squatters. The yearly round is dictated by climate and the rhythm of lambing and shearing; dingoes, rabbits and kangaroos must be controlled, and

On a cattle station in the Cloncurry region of Queensland, sunlight catches on the wings of a flock of little corellas leaving their roosts at dawn. Members of the cockatoo family, the birds are found in large numbers throughout northern Australia.

4

drought remains a potential killer. Relations within the station are still an ordered hierarchy, wool is pressed and baled by methods similar to those used more than 50 years ago, and the shearing is still carried out by itinerant gangs of skilled workers.

Sheep shearers traditionally were, and to some extent still are, the most respected group of manual workers in the country. When writers began the quest for an Australian national identity in the late 19th century, they elevated these hard-living outback itinerants to the status of folk heroes. Their exploits and way of life were immortalized in bush ballads and in the writings of the two laureates of the outback, Andrew "Banjo" Paterson—whose works include Australia's unofficial anthem, *Waltzing Matilda*—and the poet and short-story writer Henry Lawson.

Shearing was not simply a means of making money; it was a competition, with each man bidding to be the champion, or "ringer", as described in one of Paterson's poems:

The man that rung the Tubbo shed is not the ringer here,
That stripling from the Coomaside can teach him how to shear.
They turn away the ragged locks, and rip the cutter goes
And leaves a track of snowy fleece from brisket to the nose;
It's lovely how they peel it off with never stop nor stay,
They're racing for the ringer's place this year at Castlereagh.

Today, the wool shearers remain as competitive as ever, but none of the present generation are able to challenge Jackie Howe, the most celebrated of all the "guns", as the fast workers are called. In 1802, he created a world record at Alice Downs by shearing 321 sheep in a day, using hand shears.

The other outback working men to have become enshrined in Australian national mythology are the stockmen and the drovers of the cattle stations. Though there were only approximately 34,000 stations in 1980, together they constituted the dominant enterprise over nearly half of all the agricultural land in Australia, with their greatest concentration in the centre and north of the country, which, though dry, supports native grasses and shrubs that make good cattle fodder. Within this vast semi-arid area, where nearly all the water has to be pumped from deep artesian wells, there are stations as large as some countries; properties average more than 200,000 hectares in the Northern Territory as a whole, and as much as 600,000 hectares on the Barkly Tableland in the north-eastern part of the Northern Territory. Most of these stations are now owned either by Australian meat companies or by British, American and Japanese multinational concerns.

They were originally started, however, by pioneers who followed in the tracks of the outback explorers and sometimes went ahead of them, opening up virgin country on their own initiative. One of the unforeseen benefits to arise from the tragic Burke and Wills expedition of 1860–61 was that the search parties who went looking for the missing explorers returned with reports of good cattle pasture deep in the outback. Just as, a generation earlier, sheepmen had moved into the newly opened areas of the south-east, cattlemen began the long trek to the north. At first they concentrated their efforts on the state of Queensland, but by the end of the 1870s they were searching for new pastures in the north-west.

Reports of good grazing land in the Kimberleys induced Patrick Durack, patriarch of a family of Queensland cattlemen, to arrange the overland transportation of a mustering of cattle 10,000 strong over a distance of some 3,000 kilometres, from the Cooper Creek area to the Ord River. The leading groups left in May 1883 and did not reach their destination for nearly two and a half years; but though the journey had taken a heavy toll of the beasts, there were still sufficient cattle left to found six great properties from which in years to come cattle would be sent overland to the southern settlements. But even this great trek fades into insignificance when it is compared with the clearance of cattle from the Northern Territory in 1942, an operation organized to deny food to a threatened Japanese invasion force. In all, some 100,000 cattle were moved to the south, some of them walking a distance of more than 1,500 kilometres.

In spite of the introduction of new cattle strains and feeds, the sheer size of the northern stations makes careful husbandry, as practised in more temperate climes, well nigh impossible. In some areas, the intense heat of the day means that most calves born between dawn and late afternoon will not be

The driver of a two-trailer road train *(right)* pauses for a rest while transporting cattle from an outback station to a city slaughterhouse. Long distances and overwhelming heat cause some beasts to die in transit, and dead stock must be disposed of in pits *(above)* before the train reaches its destination.

able to survive their first day. Not surprisingly, some agronomists have been critical of outback cattle-rearing, describing it as exploitative and unscientific. One critic writing in the 1960s claimed that there were still stations in the more remote areas of the country where management consisted of two operations—branding cattle in order to establish ownership, and "turning off"—freighting out for sale—those cattle which could be mustered.

Outback cattle are still kept on undeveloped pasture, and when drought reduces the amount of natural fodder and the carrying capacity of the land, there is a race to round up the herd and get them to market before they die of starvation or grow too thin to fetch an economic price. The problem lies in gathering the wild cattle that roam in the stations' outer limits. In the past, mounted stockmen would track them down, manually wrestle them to the ground, and then lash the hind legs together with a rope or leather strap. "Coaches"—tractable cattle from the home pastures—would be driven up to the hobbled beast. Calmed by their docile presence, the wild bull or cow would then be untied and driven back to the stock camp. Nowadays, however, aircraft are often used in the mustering operation. Several fixed-wing aeroplanes, perhaps augmented by a helicopter, may help to drive the cattle into a mustering yard set up at the end of a long funnel constructed from hessian or other natural materials.

Until the 1960s, mustered cattle were driven to market or a railway terminal by drovers—tough men, whose reputation for rough camaraderie and drinking perhaps exceeded even that of the sheep shearers:

Now there's a trade you all know well,
It's bringing cattle over;
I'll tell you all about the time
When I became a drover.
I made a line for Queensland,
To Kempsey I did wander;
I picked up a mob of duffers there
And began as an overlander.

High living was the order of the day once the cattle had been sold and the

4

A pregnant Aborginal woman *(below)* receives medical attention aboard one of the 28 aeroplanes of the Flying Doctor Service. Operating from 14 bases nationwide, the planes can be summoned by radio to cattle station landing-strips *(right)* where they airlift patients needing hospital treatment.

drovers had been paid their wages:

In town we drain the whisky glass
And go to see the play;
We never think of being hard up
Or how to spend the day;
We sheer up to the pretty girls
Who rig themselves with grandeur,
And as long as we spend our check, my lads,
They love the overlander.

The heirs of the overlanders are the drivers of the road trains—monstrous Pullmans of the roadways, consisting of a mammoth truck towing as many as four trailers like freight-cars on tyres. Even with only two trailers, a road train may be up to 60 metres long and carry 100 cattle or 600 sheep. Meeting a road train on a lonely outback highway is an extremely nerve-racking experience, especially at night, when the first indication of the impending monster is just a distant glow on the horizon from the truck's giant headlights. With infinite slowness the glow will become larger and brighter, and the noise of the engine will gradually make itself heard. Finally, the long train will roar past with a rush of air strong enough to jostle the suspension of the stoutest car, before the trailers behind it, illuminated with strings of lights, fall away into the darkness, rising and falling with the surface of the road like some great primeval beast.

Unwelcoming at the best of times, the outback can in extreme circumstances prove a lethal enemy. Its dangers are graphically illustrated by the story of Harry Lasseter, a stocky and dark-complexioned man who, one day in March 1930, presented himself in the office of John Bailey, President of the Australian Workers' Union. He had a startling tale to tell. Twenty-three years earlier, he said, he had found a reef of gold while searching for rubies in the mountains of central Australia; seeking to return with his spoils, he had got lost, and his horses had perished one by one. He had been rescued by a surveyor named Harding, with whom he subsequently returned in search of the lost reef. They relocated it, and this time Lasseter marked its position; but when they returned to civilization, they found that their watches were running slow and consequently the bearings they had taken were incorrect. In the following years, gold was discovered in other, easier areas of the outback and, Lasseter said, he himself had joined in one of the rushes. He had temporarily put aside further plans to revisit the reef, although he continued to nurture dreams of its eventual rediscovery.

There was a certain vagueness about Lasseter's account that did not inspire much confidence, and many people have subsequently questioned whether there was any truth in it at all. But in 1930, in John Bailey's office, his story fell on appreciative ears. The other goldfields had been mined out, and the Great Depression was beginning to bite. Whatever misgivings had been expressed, a consortium of Sydney businessmen was found to provide financial backing for a new sortie in search of the reef, and a company was established to organize the quest. Funds were not lacking. When the six-man party at last set out from Alice Springs, they could call on the services of a specially designed six-wheel truck, an auxiliary lorry and a light aeroplane. In contrast to Lasseter's earlier, amateur efforts, this was the best-equipped expedition to its date in the history of Australian mineral exploration.

Whether or not Lasseter lied in his original claims, it is certain that the lat-

ter quest became an epic of endurance. The story of the next five months' adventures is a catalogue of extravagant misfortune that will only seem astonishing to those who are unfamiliar with outback travel. The aeroplane crashed on take-off on its second flight. A replacement sent out by the company directors made one successful reconnaissance, in the course of which Lasseter claimed to recognize landmarks around the reef. It then returned to the coast, the pilots refusing to make any further sorties over such dangerous territory without the security of a larger engine and petrol tank. The six-wheel truck was forced to turn back when it reached an impassable stretch of sandstone country scored by ledges as much as 100 metres deep. Lasseter, whose obsession with finding gold was matched only by his mistrust of his fellow travellers, persuaded them to return to Alice Springs. Then he pressed forward in the company of a young bushman called Paul Johns, who had attached himself to the party. Food and equipment were carried on Johns' five camels; but as the train arrived at the Petermann Ranges—the goal of their quest—unexpected rain swiftly turned the desert into a quagmire, bogging down the beasts of burden. Even without this unexpected setback, Lasseter seems to have made up his mind not to let Johns see the gold reef. Irrationally, he insisted on turning back. The two men came to blows over the issue, but Lasseter was adamant. Retracing their steps, they journeyed back some 200 kilometres to their base camp, and Lasseter, taking just two of the camels, set off again, this time on his own.

The rest of his story we know only from Aboriginal oral history and from fragmentary and heat-damaged journals and letters, buried by the prospector in caves where he had sheltered and underneath the ashes of his camp-fires. He returned to the Petermanns and rediscovered the reef. He "pegged" it, marking his claim to the gold; but before he left the site to re-establish contact with his companions and the wider world, disaster struck. As he started to unload the camels for the night's camp, the beasts bolted. They disappeared

4

over the horizon, leaving Lasseter alone in the desert with a revolver, perhaps a fortnight's supply of food, but no water. He was discovered by a wandering group of Pitjantjatjara Aboriginals. He travelled with this wild fraternity for a month or more; but relations between the tribesmen and their uninvited guest were always edgy, and his journals speak of attempts on his life as well as acts of individual kindness.

Matters came to a head when the tribe encamped for several weeks in a well-watered valley. Lasseter's plight had steadily worsened. He had been struck down by dysentery, and by the form of conjunctivitis known to the bushmen as sandy blight. He also learnt, through the Aboriginals' bush telegraph of smoke signals, that the aeroplanes he expected to be searching the area for him had not been sighted. Alone, scared, sick and sheltering in a cave, he made the mistake of shooting at some Aboriginal youths he thought had come to taunt him. Some of the tribal elders, already unsettled by his presence, then "sang" him, which meant they had cast a fatal curse. Regarding him as to all extents and purposes already dead, they withdrew all material support. Starvation threatened.

By now, Lasseter's sufferings were intense. His waistline had shrunk so that he had taken in his belt by 10 notches. He was tormented by flies and ants which, he wrote, "have nearly eaten my face away". He had almost lost the use of both eyes. In this condition, he set off with about one and a half litres of water—the most he could carry in his weakened state—to try to cover the 140 kilometres to Mount Olga, where he hoped that help would be waiting. He never got there. It was just 55 kilometres from the cave to where his bones

At Mable Downs cattle station on Western Australia's Kimberley Plateau, a cook prepares damper, unleavened bread baked in a camp oven buried in hot embers. A traditional part of the outback worker's diet, damper is still a staple in remote areas.

were discovered by the relief party.

Subsequently, several expeditions tried to retrace his tracks in the Petermanns, but none met with success. If Lasseter was telling the truth, then somewhere in the dry mountains, undisturbed by all the mineral exploration activity of the post-war years, his reef still waits to be rediscovered.

Lasseter's story indicates vividly the difficulties and dangers of mineral exploration in the outback, especially for those foolhardy enough to try going it alone. Yet the rewards in many cases have been more than commensurate with the efforts involved. Scattered through the Australian hinterland are such successful and long-established mining centres as the opal fields of Coober Pedy; the lead, zinc and silver mines at Broken Hill in New South Wales; and Kalgoorlie in Western Australia, once the scene of a famous gold rush and again in the 1980s a major centre for the mineral.

The mineral boom of the post-war years brought a new breed of men to the outback. It was pioneered less by the prospectors of the old school than by university-trained geologists, whose educated guesses, supported by full-scale surveys financed by mining companies, proved right often enough to encourage the belief that Australia's remote inland might be an unexploited treasurehouse. The list of their successes is long and include many different natural resources, from iron ore, nickel and bauxite in Western Australia, through copper, uranium, iron and petroleum in the Northern Territory, to uranium, lead, zinc, silver, gas and bauxite in Queensland. Yet the harsh rules of outback living had not changed for the new prospectors, despite the influx of all the up-to-date technology; accounts of mining workers meeting their death strolling away from the protected environment of the camp and losing their way still appear with tragic frequency in Australian newspapers.

The outback's other great resource is empty space, an asset most spectacularly tapped by the rocket range which stretches for thousands of kilometres from Woomera, in South Australia, to the Indian Ocean coastline south of Broome. For much of the way this vast testing-ground passes over totally uninhabited desert, flat and open enough for scientists to have little difficulty in tracking down strayed missiles and lost parts by taking sight checks from the air. Those few sheep stations that actually lie within the range's edges were thoughtfully provided with concrete shelters by the Australian government, which shared the cost of constructing the range with Britain. The missile-testing and satellite-tracking carried out from the range have mercifully not required the shelters' use; so far they have only seen service as supplementary byres or milking-sheds. More recently, the Australian government has joined with the government of the United States to run defence bases whose functions are to monitor missile launches and nuclear explosions, and to provide a military early warning system; one of these lies in the heart of the outback at Pine Gap, just 27 kilometres south-west of Alice Springs.

The social infrastructure that links the widely scattered population of the outback is necessarily limited by the great distances involved, but it includes two unique features developed to conquer the problems of remoteness: the Flying Doctor Service and the School of the Air. Each is an attempt to bring basic social services to citizens who may live as much as 1,500 kilometres from the nearest city, and hundreds of kilometres from the closest hospital or school. Until well into the 20th century, most of the outback children were educated by their parents or were self-taught, and commonplace illnesses such as appendicitis were often fatal, since it took days and sometimes weeks to reach medical aid.

It was to cope with situations such as this, and also to help the people of the outback to communicate with their neighbours, that the Reverend John Flynn set up the Flying Doctor Service. Ordained as a Presbyterian minister in 1911, Flynn had experienced for himself the isolation of the settlers when he travelled on missionary work throughout the bush. With the help of his church and other missionaries, he established a small hospital, staffed with nurses, at Oodnadatta in South Australia in 1912. It proved so successful that he received many requests to build other hospitals. Since the construction

Stockmen at Killarney in the Northern Territory have a meal in the canteen. At 4,000 square kilometres, Killarney is only average-sized for a cattle station. Even so, it houses a community of 60 and boasts a complex of living quarters and offices with its own school and street lighting at night.

and operating costs were so high as to be prohibitive, Flynn set out to provide medical aid for people in the bush with the help of aeroplanes.

The idea of using aircraft to solve the problem came from a young medical student called Clifford Peel, who outlined his plan to Flynn shortly before going off to fight in World War I as a pilot with the Australian Flying Corps. Peel was killed in action before his idea became reality. In fact it took until 1928 to inaugurate the service—a delay caused by the need to raise money and develop a rudimentary radio network that would link up the outlying homesteads. Money was eventually raised by donation; the communications problem was solved by an amateur radio enthusiast who developed a bicycle-powered Morse code transmitter. By 1929, the first six sets were installed in properties within a 500-kilometre radius of the Service's first headquarters, at Cloncurry in Queensland. The users could receive spoken

messages from the radio station, but they had to send their replies in Morse code, generating the necessary power by operating a pedal-driven dynamo.

By this time, Flynn had recruited his first doctor, a surgeon from Sydney who, in the inaugural year, flew almost 28,000 kilometres in a de Havilland biplane, attending some 250 emergency calls. The service was an immediate success and rapidly expanded. By the beginning of the 1980s, it had grown into a nationwide network of 14 bases equipped with 28 hospital aeroplanes and employing a staff of more than a hundred. In 1981, the service transported more than 9,000 patients on evacuation and repatriation flights; most of them were Aboriginals.

To simplify the administration, non-emergency calls from the homesteads are received at scheduled "surgery" times; they are then transmitted via the radio station to a hospital, where a doctor and a nurse diagnose the symptoms. After diagnosis, the doctor prescribes a

4

course of do-it-yourself treatment or, if necessary, arranges for the patient to be evacuated for hospital care. To facilitate therapy, each station linked to the Flying Doctor network is equipped with a comprehensive medical kit, with each item numbered for identification. The doctor simply tells the caller what number medicine to use, and how to administer it.

The School of the Air began in 1950 under the aegis of the older service, and used the two-way radio transmitter and receiver at the Flying Doctor base in Alice Springs. By the early 1980s, it was a well-organized programme, receiving funds from state governments and broadcasting to some 20,000 pupils scattered over distances of almost 2.25 million square kilometres. Teachers speak simultaneously over two channels, to ensure good reception at homesteads both near and far. Each time they ask a question, the pupils competing to get their answer in first may live as much as 1,500 kilometres apart. Once a year, largely at the School's expense, the children are brought together in order to meet their teachers. Primary-age children rendezvous in Alice Springs; older pupils gather in one of the large cities, thereby broadening their experience of Australia and the world, as well as learning to put the faces to the voices that have become so familiar to them in the course of the preceding 12 months.

Other social events in the outback's calendar are few and far between. There are race meetings for amateur jockeys—the most famous is held each June at Brunette Downs in the Northern Territory—and rodeos in country towns or on the large cattle stations. Popular sports at these rough-and-ready agricultural shows include steer-

riding—judged on the length of time each contestant can stay on the bucking animal—buckjumping, in which unbroken stallions take the place of the steers, and camp drafting, which involves racing to round up small groups of cattle. But the most keenly followed activity is woodchopping, in which axemen and timbergetters compete with each other in chopping and sawing through timber logs, using axes so finely honed that they could probably shave with them.

In Darwin, they hold an annual regatta for rafts made out of empty beer cans, always in plentiful supply in that thirsty northern metropolis. But the event that best sums up the spirit of the outback in all its dry irony is held in Alice Springs. It is whimsically known as the Henley-on-Todds regatta— Henley from the celebrated boating centre on England's River Thames, Todd from Alice's own river. The joke is that this river is almost always dry; the water course only fills after rare heavy rainfall. To complete the irony, the organizers each year take out insurance against rain, for water would spoil the whole purpose of the event, which is for competing teams to run along the bed of the river in yachts which have no bottom. Alternatively, sculls race along rails, propelled by rowers digging their oars into sand. This preposterous and energetically pursued exercise has now become a major tourist attraction, and draws visitors not just from the outback itself but also from the southern cities. In its unpretentious way it says a great deal about the way in which the people of Australia have come to terms with the harsh and unforgiving hinterland of their country— not with fear and not with awe so much as with a dry and stoical humour.

A helicopter, used to round up cattle from the hills, hovers in swirling dust over several thousand beasts waiting to be driven to the stockyards.

AN ABORIGINAL REVIVAL

Sole occupants of the Australian continent for tens of thousands of years, the Aboriginals came close to destruction within a century of the arrival of European settlers. Their numbers declined, they were driven from their traditional lands and their lifestyle was largely destroyed. Over the past decades, however, their fortunes have revived: the population is now rising, and legislation has restored at least some of their territory.

Symptomatic of the new, optimistic mood is the "outstation" movement. Several hundred clans, mainly in Western Australia and the Northern Territory, have formed tribal communities that live as much as possible in the traditional manner. No longer nomadic, they accept such compromises as the need to herd some livestock and make craft goods for sale. But as these pictures—taken on Arnhem Land outstations—show, they continue to practise their old hunting skills and preserve their culture through painting, dance and song.

Watched by his son and a lively pet possum, the Aboriginal artist George Milpurrur paints an episode from his clan's history on a strip of eucalyptus bark. His colours are made from such natural materials as ground ochre, clay and charcoal, and are applied with a soft twig that serves as a brush.

A detail of a much larger painting by
Milpurrur shows clan ancestors
meeting animals from the Dreamtime—
the legendary period when the world was
made. Bark paintings by leading artists
command high prices among city
collectors, providing a valuable source
of revenue for some outstations.

123

Walking into a breeze to keep the flames behind him, a spear-carrying man lights dry undergrowth with a firestick of rolled bark. Setting controlled fires to burn off scrub is a vital safety measure in the dry season, when hunters could be trapped by accidental conflagrations.

Large strips of bark draped over a framework of branches make a house big enough for several families to share. In the past, when Aboriginals were nomadic, they built only temporary shelters. Today's stations are permanent settlements, and the houses are used all year round.

A family on the Yathalamarra station tend pumpkins, courgettes and onions in a garden partly sheltered by trees from the fierce sun. Traditionally, Aboriginals only gathered wild plants as vegetables, but crop-growing has been adopted by some outstations as a convenient additional food source.

Carrying her son on her shoulders, a woman from the Nangala outstation walks home from a freshwater swamp with the proceeds of a morning's food-gathering: a long-necked turtle and two water-lilies. The turtle will be roasted over hot stones, gutted and cut into chunks; the lilies will be eaten raw.

Near Maningrida, a man fishing in the open sea uses a traditional pronged spear to increase his catch, so far consisting of two flat moonfish and a large mullet. Fish are plentiful off the Arnhem Land coast, but catching them requires courage, because the waters are infested with crocodiles.

To the deep, droning notes of the didgeridoo—a hollowed tree-trunk played as a musical instrument—Aboriginals in the Roper Valley perform dances passed down through generations. The dancers may imitate animal movements, as in the kangaroo dance *(below)*, or re-enact tribal battles from the distant past in spear dances *(right)*. Such secular dances have always played an important part in ceremonial gatherings known as corroborees. Aboriginal men also practise other, sacred dances never seen in public—or by the women of the clan.

A couple relax in deck chairs in a
Perth park while a swimsuit-clad
woman lies in sun-soaked oblivion
behind them. A sunny climate has
made Australians an outdoor people,
as enthusiastic about the non-
competitive pleasures of sunbathing
as about sport.

PLEASURE AS A WAY OF LIFE

Australians enjoy more leisure time than their counterparts in most other countries. In addition to the four to five weeks' paid vacation that the average worker expects each year, there are about a dozen public holidays, which are usually scheduled for a Monday so that employees can look forward to a long weekend. Then there is that other national institution, the "sickie"—a day off sick, which has been regularized in some occupations to a maximum number of permitted days a year. It is amazing how often the "sickie" turns out to coincide with the mid-week horse races, or with an important Test (international) cricket match, or the Melbourne Cup horse race. All these official and unofficial holidays act as relief valves from the monotony and pressures of modern full-time work, and though they might be the despair of economists and businessmen, they are regarded by most Australians as an inalienable right.

The recreation patterns have been changing recently for the beneficiaries of these generous amounts of spare time. In the past, public leisure activities tended to be male-oriented, gregarious and focused on sport, drinking and gambling on "the dogs, the trots and the races"—greyhound racing, trotting and conventional horse racing. Now, however, participation is the major theme. Instead of herding as anonymous spectators into some huge sporting crowd, Australians now are more likely to jump into cars at a weekend and fan out to a variety of more individual pursuits: a day spent at the beach, bush picnics, camping, maybe some sailing or surfing, a party at night or a visit to the local beer garden on Sunday "arvo", meaning afternoon.

The new leisure pattern is also less masculine in emphasis. The trend is evident in sport, in which nearly every event, from motor racing to wrestling to football, is now opening to women, who have gained admittance to that bastion of masculinity, the surf lifesaving club, and even forced their way into the jockey clubs. But the most dramatic invasion of a traditional male preserve has taken place in the pubs and bars of the nation. Once, drinking was an almost all-male activity; the pubs used to be crowded with shouting, swearing, "'ave another beer mate" drinkers, and exuded what the British travel writer Jan Morris described as "a frightening sense of male collusion". Women were banned from the bars or consigned to sit in poky little Ladies' Lounges at the back of the pub. There are still a few bloodhouses, as the rowdier institutions are called, patronized exclusively by men; but these days women drink wherever they please and the typical pub has carpeted bars, an entertainment lounge and an open-air beer garden where the men and women drink together.

Some 64 per cent of women and 83 per cent of men in Australia consume alcohol, and for both sexes beer is still the most popular brew. Their drinking habits, though, have mellowed somewhat. Australians used to boast about how strong their beer was, but in the mid-1980s there was a major shift in the market to low-alcohol beers—a move perhaps encouraged by the introduction of random blood-alcohol tests on motorists by the police.

At the same time, there has also been an astonishing growth in the consumption of Australian wines. Once dismissed by the experts as ''plonk'', the vintages of the Barossa and Clare Valleys in South Australia, the Hunter Valley in New South Wales and other vinicultural centres have gained an international reputation, and every pub and drive-in cellar has wine bottles, casks and flagons for sale. Virtually every newspaper—even the afternoon tabloids—has its own wine columnist, while magazines such as the *National Times* carry wine supplements, wine guides and pages of advertisments.

The increasing affluence of the post-war era has created a surge of enthusiasm for new and expensive outdoor activities, especially such watersports as skin-diving, water-skiing, yachting and power-boating. At weekends, Sydney Harbour is crammed with yachts and craft of every conceivable shape and size; and the lakes and estuaries of the coast host all kinds of mooring from backyard piers to marinas where the boats have to be stacked like trays by fork-lift trucks in open, multi-storey warehouses, because of the lack of space at sea-level. Windsurfing and hang-gliding have also become popular. The most exclusive outdoor activity is skiing, which even comfortably remunerated middle-class Australians find expensive, despite the fact—much touted by tourist brochures—that the Snowy Mountains have more skiable snowfields than Switzerland.

The change in the economics of leisure is noticeable in many other areas. People in their teens and twenties earn enough to pay substantial sums for a ticket to watch the world's top rock bands and entertainers. One of the main venues for such events is the circular 20,000-capacity Sydney Entertainment Centre, built by the New South Wales Labor government and the most important new public building in the city since the construction of the Sydney Opera House.

The new wealth is visible even on the streets—for example, in the number of ordinary family cars that are equipped with towbars to cart a camping trailer, caravan, boat or trail bike around the countryside. Off-road driving has become popular, with sales of four-wheel drive vehicles soaring and most suburban streets adorned with at least one wide-wheeled, multi-striped, imported Land Cruiser, Prairie, Jackaroo, Patrol Waggon or Range Rover. A lot of them never leave the bitumen, of course; but they look as though they could if the

Correctly padded and gloved for a casual afternoon cricket match, a young batsman takes guard in front of a watchful tyro wicket-keeper. Cricket is an early enthusiasm for many Australians, and is played very seriously at school level.

In a style befitting a national hero, the
cricketer Dennis Lillee makes his
farewell appearance during a one-day
international match against the West
Indies in 1984. Considered by many
to be the greatest fast bowler of his
day, Lillee cowed batsmen with the
speed and hostility of his deliveries.

owners were game enough to risk damaging the repayments. Even more in evidence are the private swimming pools which grace one in 10 Australian homes. To take the chore out of pool-cleaning, an Australian team invented the world's first automatic cleaner, the "creepy crawly", which moves over the pool floor and sucks up grime and dirt.

Other elements of Australian leisure have remained constant. Visiting the homes of friends and relatives, often unannounced, just to "have a chat" is a confirmed habit; Australians will happily drive 50 kilometres to see the family or go to a party. In some country areas, the old ritual still exists whereby the men stay together at one end of the room, yarning around a keg of beer, while the women chat amongst themselves down at the other. In the cities and larger towns, however, there is no segregation and a freewheeling sexuality is apparent. Australia has cast off most of its notorious puritanism, which once made the "wowser", or killjoy, a familiar figure in public life: the nation now has sex shops, R (restricted) rated films, a plethora of sex magazines, including women's monthlies with nude male centrefolds, and some of the most straightforwardly sexual television advertising in the world.

Gambling is also as prevalent as ever, though the forms it takes have

THE BIG RACE

With the city skyline in the background, jockeys gallop for home in the Melbourne Cup.

On the first Tuesday of each November, some 80,000 people crowd into Flemington Race Course for the country's most prestigious horse race, the Melbourne Cup. Initiated in 1861, the two-mile classic provides an opportunity for displays of racecourse elegance as well as for resolute punting. Off the track it brings the nation to a temporary halt, as the High Court goes into recess, Parliament stops its debates, and an estimated third of the nation tunes in to follow the action on radio or television.

A row of smartly dressed ladies display suitable decorum in the members' enclosure at Flemington.

A flamboyant pair of racegoers study form in the paddock.

changed. Australians, it is claimed, are the heaviest gamblers in the world and will bet on flies crawling up a window-pane. The state governments, under whose legislation gambling falls, foster rather than discourage, the compulsion. They have introduced variations of Lotto such as Scratch Lotto—a form of the game in which the numbers on the card are revealed by scratching away opaque coatings—in addition to the old state-run lotteries. They also run off-course betting through totalisator agencies (the "tote", a mechanical device which shows the amount of bets placed on a race and divides the winnings equally, is an Australian invention). Casinos, which were once banned throughout the continent, have been introduced legally at places like West Point in Tasmania and illegally in the baccarat clubs and gaming houses of Melbourne and Sydney, which survive only because the authorities choose to look the other way.

Poker machines—called one-armed bandits—were banned in the states of Victoria and Queensland, but in New South Wales they actually form the financial backbone of the huge sports and Returned Servicemen's League (RSL or "rissole") social clubs. These popular institutions, which are now open to virtually anyone who wishes to join, often boast bars, restaurants, games rooms, dance floors and showbusiness entertainers as well as the ubiquitous "pokies". Playing the pokies is an obsession that cuts across gender, generation and class; in the clubs, which have replaced pubs as the chief social centres in many suburbs and towns, the rows of one-armed bandits are often attended by battalions of women who, cigarette in mouth and beer in hand, spend hours feeding 20 and 10-cent

During a wood-chopping contest in Canberra, brawny axemen race to cut through upright logs. Starting at the top, contestants move down a plank each time they cut through a section of the timber. The winner is the first to reach the ground.

pieces into the insatiable machines.

In the face of stiff competition from the pokies, Australia's traditional gambling game, Two-up, is dying out. Besides, because of betting abuses in the past, it is illegal. To play it, a circle of people surrounds a central spinner and bets on whether two pennies, spun from a flat piece of wood called the kip, will turn up heads or tails; if the coins are unmatched, the spinner then keeps the stakes. Today, the game survives mainly in army camps and among ex-servicemen as a nostalgic diversion on Anzac Day. Many more people gamble on horse racing, even though they may never visit a racecourse; a poll taken in the 1970s concluded that one Australian in six bets on the horses at least once a month and an additional one in four had an occasional flutter.

Although the pubs and clubs are the most favoured places to spend an evening out, night-time leisure, as in most Western countries, is dominated by television. According to surveys, nearly all Australian families own a television set; seven out of 10 Australians watch TV programmes regularly; and three in 10 watch almost every night. Almost every home has a radio, and the advent of the "trannie" (portable radio) and portable cassette player means that young Australians have taken to carrying their music with them wherever they go, which has prompted a rash of new anti-noise laws.

Then there are such predominantly night-time pursuits as going to the pictures and dancing. But here again there has been a move from the communal to the domestic. Australians have taken to home video films with a vengeance; video parties are all the rage and just about every suburb, town and village in the nation sports a video rental shop.

As a result, cinema audiences are getting smaller and smaller, while the once-popular drive-ins are closing down everywhere because of the lack of customers. The old-time dance palais has also disappeared, and has been replaced by discotheques, clubs and live-music venues, in which young people tend to dance alone rather than with somebody; even if they have a partner they perform separately, facing the band rather than each other.

For weekends and holidays, Australians love to "get away from it all". Some 80 per cent of Australians spend their vacations away from home. The majority stay in Australia, usually travelling by car and staying in motels, camping grounds or camper vans, or else with friends or family. A predominantly urban people, Australians like getting out into the bush, and a Sunday car drive, followed by a bush picnic, is almost a national institution.

For the more energetic hiker, there are splendid national parks and state forests along the coastline and scattered throughout the interior. Most have camp-sites, which may be booked up months in advance, especially for Easter and other public holidays. The distances involved do not deter vacationers; it is common for Sydneysiders to make an overnight drive of about 1,000 kilometres in order to reach the Queensland Gold Coast beaches, or to drive 450 kilometres to the Snowy Mountains trout streams for a weekend's fishing. Many Australians own "weekenders"—holiday cottages—on the coast or out in the bush.

The same readiness to travel for pleasure can be seen in the extraordinary number of Australians who go touring overseas: nearly a million a year, according to the Australian Bureau of Statistics. Some of them go for their holidays to places such as Bali, which is in fact closer for Western Australians to visit than the east coast of their own country. Package tours to the Pacific islands, the Philippines and Hong Kong are often a cheaper bargain than flights from the southern cities to the holiday resorts on Queensland. Large numbers of Australians also make the Grand Tour of Britain and Europe. Certain streets in London are lined with second-hand camper vans offered for sale by Australian owners seeking to raise the price of the air fare home; and along Europe's hitch-hiking routes, backpackers sporting the Aussie flag are a regular part of the scenery.

The appeal of globe-trotting to the young Australians shows no sign of abating. A prolonged period of foreign travel is a once-in-a-lifetime initiation rite for many school and university leavers before they settle down to start careers and families. Others choose to save up to travel after several years of salary-earning, seeking something other than their comfortable, basically insular world. If Australia has become more cosmopolitan and more sophisticated over the years, then part of the reason is the breakdown of that geographic loneliness which once condemned Australian culture to parochialism.

In one field at least, the charge of parochialism has never been applicable. Considering the small population of Australia, its record in international sport is little short of astonishing. For years it was the pacesetter in world swimming and it has an almost unrivalled record in tennis. The nation won the Davis Cup—the premier international team event in tennis—19 times between 1939 and 1983, and produced

37 Wimbledon champions—including doubles partners—up to 1982. The roll-call of tennis stars includes John Bromwich, Lew Hoad, Ken Rosewall, Rod Laver, John Newcombe, Margaret Court and the part-Aboriginal Evonne Cawley, née Goolagong.

Australia is also one of the world's great cricketing nations. It has won the Ashes, as the England–Australia test match series is known, as many times as England, from whom it learnt the game; and in Don Bradman, it produced probably the finest batsman the game has ever known. It has had world champions in motor racing, squash, horse riding, shooting, athletics and boxing. In the early 1980s, it led the world in Rugby League football and surf-riding, and in 1983 it won the world's most coveted yachting prize, the Americas' Cup, which the United

TRADITIONS OF BRAWN AND BRAVERY

Lifesavers carrying lifelines march in the opening parade of the annual Sydney surf carnival.

Through the height of the Australian summer, the nation's 236 surf lifesaving clubs—bands of volunteer lifeguards organized to help swimmers and surfers in distress—hold a colourful series of weekend carnivals at venues around the coast. Those held on the beaches of Sydney are the most famous, attracting large crowds with their unique pageantry and their thrilling displays of split-second teamwork.

Each carnival begins with a parade in which the lifesavers bear their club banners. Then there are staged rescue and resuscitation exercises, judged on speed of execution. But for the spectators the high points of the day are usually the surfboat races, in which crews in rowing boats compete against each other and the waves to round marker buoys beyond the surf line and return furiously to shore.

Competing in the surfboat race, a crew of five struggle to pull their craft through the pounding breakers to a distant marker buoy.

A portly lifeguard stands to attention with his club banner.

States had held for 132 years. No other country of similar size can boast such an impressive sporting record.

The stars who have managed to put Australia on the sporting map are the product of a longstanding national sporting tradition that at any one time involves literally millions of ordinary Australians. A series of Gallup polls conducted shortly after World War II discovered that about four Australians in 10 regularly participated in a sport, and three out of four watched it. In schools, children still take such an interest in games that head teachers sometimes have to discourage them from becoming obsessive.

The nation is of course blessed with an ideal climate and environment for physical exercise. The Australians can swim in the sea nearly all year round, except in Tasmania and perhaps Victoria, where aficionados of surfing and sail-boarding have to wear wetsuits in the colder months. In such a large and sparsely settled continent, there is plenty of space for outdoor pursuits, and the long, warm summers enable people to indulge their love of outdoor sports as much as they like. The aridity of the interior is a drawback, but most country towns have an Olympic-size swimming pool—and maybe also an 18-hole golf course, a race track, a showground, several cricket and football fields, tennis courts, squash courts, indoor gymnasiums, a greyhound and trotting track, a speedway, roads with special cycle lanes, walking trails, a roller skating track, and a shooting range. In the cities, these facilities are augmented by premises that cater for the latest products of the physical fitness cult—jazz exercise, yoga, martial arts, saunas, bodybuilding. Some of the health and "jazzercise" clubs are situated on the top floor of city buildings, so that busy executives can have a workout in the middle of the day, followed by lunch at a health food restaurant attached to the club.

While the trend is towards individual participation, traditional spectator sports such as cricket and football still generate enormous interest. Since the 1970s they have become heavily commercialized. Rugby League players and even referees carry the names of sponsors on the backs of their jerseys, and football grounds are festooned with advertisements for cigarette brands. Cricket resisted the grosser aspects of commercialism until 1977, when media magnate Kerry Packer signed up most of Australia's Test cricketers together with other outstanding world players, and paid them to compete in tournaments wearing brightly coloured uniforms (green and gold for Australia) in place of the traditional all-white gear. The customary red ball was replaced by a white one for easier viewing under floodlights—themselves a radical departure from convention. The Packer circus only endured for two years, but some of the innovations it sponsored have now entered the mainstream of Australian cricket.

Football in all its Australian variety remains the favourite sport for spectators. Four different versions are played: soccer, two versions of Rugby—Rugby Union, the running-and-passing game played 15 a side, and Rugby League, the pared-down professional game with 13 men in each team—and Australian Rules, an indigenous version of football which is played by 18-strong teams on an oversized pitch. Aussie Rules, which focuses on spectacular high-kicking, marking and hand-passing, dominates the southern states and has by far the

largest and most fanatical following of the four games. In Victoria, the performance of the clubs belonging to the 11-team league is a matter of intense and passionate concern to the 150,000 highly partisan spectators who attend matches each Saturday, and once a year the city of Melbourne virtually stops for the VFL (Victorian Football League) Grand Final, which attracts crowds of more than 100,000 people.

As Australian society has changed, so have its sporting heroes. Once it used to produce world champions from social groups who were fighting their way up the social scale: two of Australia's most famous folklore heroes are Les Darcy and Dave Sands, middleweight boxers who were from Irish and Aboriginal backgrounds respectively. But its heroes now tend to come from middle-class stock and excel in cool, technical skills, such as motor racing,

in which the nation has produced world champions in Jack Brabham and Alan Jones, and surfboard riding, which is now in competition with the traditional surf lifesaving movement as Australia's national sport.

The switch is symbolic. The lifesaving clubs—voluntary organizations dedicated to helping swimmers in distress—tend to be authoritarian and heavily masculine, based on one particular beach. In their rituals of mateyness and team discipline, they rehearse the movement's working-class origins. But since the beginning of the 1970s, they have lost many members to the more freewheeling and individualistic cult of surfboard riding, aimed at self-fulfilment rather than community service. Once, any male teenager growing up in a beachside suburb would have naturally gravitated towards the local surf club. Now, beachside youngsters, male and female, are more likely to buy surfboards and spend their time driving up and down the coast in borrowed cars in search of good waves. No better example could be found of the changes that have occurred in Australia—from group activities to individual pursuits, from discipline to freedom, from working-class to middle-class, from the authentically Australian to the stylishly imported. And it is the new trend, with its sense of glamour and social mobility, which most attracts the support of the media.

The media in Australia are in the main commercially run, and ownership of the principal outlets is heavily concentrated. Four powerful chains dominate the nation's television, press and radio. Just three of them—John Fairfax Limited, Rupert Murdoch's News Corporation, and the Herald & Weekly Times Limited—own every daily newspaper in the state capital cities. Together with the fourth chain, Consolidated Press, they control eight of the nation's 15 city commercial TV stations, most of the suburban press, nearly all the national magazines, and a large slice of Australian radio, putting them among the biggest corporations in all of Australia. With the introduction of Australia's domestic satellite in 1985 and the development of cable and subscription television, they can channel their programmes into even the remotest outback home, and are likely to extend their influence still further.

In theory, the power of the private media chains is balanced by the Australian Broadcasting Commission, a government-financed statutory authority that operates 10 television stations and 123 radio stations. The ABC is obliged by charter to take an even-handed

Entrants in Darwin's annual Beer Can Regatta, held off Mindil Beach, watch from a vessel built entirely of beer cans as a similarly fashioned pedal boat passes by. Construction materials are always ready to hand, for Darwinians exceed the national average by downing some 230 litres of beer a year.

approach to politics and social issues, but all its programmes are aimed upmarket at minority-interest audiences, generally commanding much smaller figures than the commercial networks. It is also outnumbered. In Adelaide, for example, there are three ABC radio stations and one ABC TV channel in competition against five commercial radio stations and three commercial TV channels.

The concentration of media ownership has inevitably led to criticism, particularly among Labor Party supporters who raise charges of political bias; only twice this century has any major daily newspaper endorsed Labor for a federal election. Another common complaint, directed particularly at the TV stations, is that many programmers aim at the lowest common denominator in public taste—hence the common perception that the best viewing to be found on Australian TV is the advertisements, which are often irreverent, sexy and imaginative. Although in 1981 the average household turned its television set on for roughly 32 hours a week, the Australian Broadcasting Tribunal has consistently found high levels of discontent among viewers. A Melbourne survey in 1975 found that 59 per cent of respondents were dissatisfied with their programmes and only

36 per cent were satisfied; an advertising survey in 1977 found that the main problems of concern to Australians were, first, high prices; second, strikes; and third, the poor quality of television programmes.

As a result, there are those who claim that the products of the Australian media are less interesting than the people who run them. The most celebrated of these is Rupert Murdoch, Australia's best-known media magnate. A part-

heir to the newspaper chain built up by his father, Murdoch began his career with the Adelaide *News*. In 1964, displaying the business acumen which has characterized his career ever since, he used the secure financial base provided by the *News* to set up *The Australian*, the first genuinely national daily paper. To solve the problem of distribution in such a large country, Murdoch based the paper in Canberra and flew the news plates out to the distant state ca-

pitals each night; later, new technology was used to print the paper simultaneously in several cities.

A strike called by the newspapers' journalists in 1975 to protest editorial interference by the management badly damaged *The Australian*'s circulation, which fell from 153,000 in 1974 to 110,000 four years later. But by that time, Murdoch had moved into television, mining and the airline business, and developed an international media

At a neighbourhood social gathering in Perth, guests cluster round the barbecue to check on the progress of their sausages and steaks. A hospitable climate and comfortable living standards combine to make alfresco parties a much-enjoyed part of the Australian summer.

interest. In 1969, he bought the ailing *Sun* in England. By deliberately "going under" its rivals in terms of sex and sensationalism, with a topless pin-up girl on page 3 of the paper daily, he managed to boost its circulation from 950,000 to 4 million. He had already acquired the *News of the World*, Britain's largest-selling Sunday newspaper, and later added the venerable London *The Times* and *Sunday Times*, both at the other end of the market.

Murdoch also turned his sights on the United States. In New York, an eclectic series of acquisitions included the radical *Village Voice*, the mouthpiece of bohemian Greenwich Village, and the mass-circulation *New York Post*. In the latter's case, however, the results of his stewardship were ambiguous. With a policy of brash and sensational news coverage, he lifted the *Post*'s circulation, but at the same time he could not attract sufficient advertisers. According to one local paper, a buyer for one of New York's most prestigious stores told him: "Rupert, Rupert, your readers are our shoplifters."

Murdoch is not the only Australian media tycoon to have achieved international celebrity. Kerry Packer is another such. Like Murdoch, Packer had inherited a media group from his father. The legacy included TV Channel 9 in Melbourne and Sydney, which he has expanded and consolidated, largely from the enormous profits generated after the introduction of colour TV in Australia in 1975. One of his publishing ventures is a women's monthly magazine called *Cleo*, containing sealed sections which, when opened along the dotted line, reveal sexually explicit articles and illustrations. Apart from these ventures and the cricket circus (which he started when the Austra-

lian Cricket Board refused to give his television network exclusive rights to coverage of a Test series), Packer has invested heavily in mineral exploration, property development and gambling ventures such as Lotto.

The export of honest-to-goodness vulgarity by Australia's press magnates has done little for Australia's international cultural reputation, yet the fact is that not since the turn of the century has there been such as efflorescence of the arts in Australia. The 1890s saw a tremendous upsurge of nationalism, which was reflected in the development of identifiable national movements in literature, painting and drama. The growth of an authentic Australian voice was particularly apparent in its literature: this was the age of the bush balladists who published in the *Bulletin* magazine, including Banjo Paterson, who wrote the ballad *The Man from Snowy River*, a well-loved anthology piece that was used as the basis for a feature film in 1982. It was also the time of Henry Lawson, probably Australia's finest short-story writer, and of novelists such as Joseph Furphy, the author of the picaresque diary–novel *Such is Life*.

In the following decades, however, Australia's artistic voice faltered. By the 1950s, Australian culture was essentially a client of the larger English-speaking democracies, with most of its books, films, television programmes and popular music being imported secondhand from Britain or the United States. There was no lack of native energy and talent in Australia itself, but the public in general was suspicious of original creation blossoming in their midst, tending to denigrate or patronize any home-made artistic products.

A 15-metre-high Christmas tree stands behind a charity collecting box in Sydney's Martin Place. Although Christmas arrives down under at the height of summer, Australians still celebrate it in northern European style, even sending cards showing robins chirping in the snow.

Another problem to be taken into account was that the audience for culture was not a large one. It was a time when the total population of Australia was only about 7.5 million—rather less than that of London.

The sheer lack of people and the depressing philistinism of much of Australian life during this period made many artists leave the country in order to pursue their careers in the great metropolitan centres overseas. Among them were painters Sydney Nolan, William Dobell, Arthur Boyd and Russell Drysdale, who were creating what was later to be labelled the "Australian School". In the field of performing arts, Robert Helpmann was in London developing his career as a dancer and, later, as a choreographer, and Joan Sutherland was building a reputation

5

as one of the world's great opera singers. Malcolm Williamson, the composer, and Ray Lawler, the playwright, also went off to England so that they could make names for themselves.

But many creative talents, especially the writers, chose to stay on and fight for recognition in their homeland. By the 1960s, A. D. Hope—an academic poet in the classical tradition—R. D. Fitzgerald and Judith Wright were publishing contemporary poetry, and their work was being included in school syllabuses. Hal Porter had established his reputation as a formidable short-story writer and a virtuoso of language. Australia's foremost literary talent, Patrick White, had returned from London soon after World War II and was writing his earlier novels and plays, many of them, such as *The Tree of Man* and *Voss*, set in a bush landscape. Younger novelists such as Randolph Stow, Thea Astley, Peter Mathers and Thomas Keneally were beginning to have their work published. The first significant Australian plays and films were coming out.

It was an exciting and challenging time for artists, a period of adventure and breakthrough, but the audience, generally, remained small and comparatively unsophisticated. If you were a painter, a film maker or a writer, you were a member of a minority battling desperately against what one Australian commentator, Ronald Conway, decided to call *The Great Australian Stupor*—the title of a book he wrote on the nation. The drone of the yahoo and the philistine was still to be heard throughout the land.

Things were changing, however, for the Australians. The 1960s and 1970s were a period of economic expansion, high employment, increasing leisure

On location amid sand dunes outside Sydney, a camera crew prepares to shoot a scene for a film about Phar Lap, a legendary racehorse of the 1930s. The renaissance of the cinema industry dates from 1969 when the Australian Film Commission was formed; in the 1970s some 200 features were made.

and growing national self-confidence. The historian H. D. Nicolson has described it as an age of democratic imperialism in which "dominating scale, luxurious finish and costly embellishment were necessary for the friendly flattery of the two rulers, people and leaders." The Sydney Opera House, most of the new arts complexes in the capital cities, and much of the city of Canberra itself were built during these two decades. Economic prosperity in a country is often associated with an access of cultural energy, mainly because people have more time and money to spend on the arts, and Australia was no exception to the general rule.

At the same time, the nation's isolation from the outside world was suddenly broken by a massive immigration programme which attracted millions of Britons and other Europeans to its shores. Cheaper air fares and technological developments in the media—colour television sets, the cassette player, satellite communications—helped the process. State-administered censorship virtually disappeared, allowing artists to create work as lively and irreverent as that produced in London or New York. A continent hanging off the southern half of the globe, which expatriate writer Murray Sayle had described as "As Far As You Can Go", suddenly found it had become part of the global village.

The effects of all these changes were to transform Australia from a cultural backwater into a major participant in the international world of the arts. Few people, for example, could have foreseen in the 1960s that in little more than a decade the Australian film industry would become one of the most visible of all national cinemas. Aided partly by finance from the government and by patronage, including the setting up of the Australian Film Development Corporation and the introduction of tax benefit schemes for film investors, the industry has created works as various as *Picnic at Hanging Rock*, *Gallipoli*, *Breaker Morant*, *Newsfront*, *The Man From Snowy River*, *My Brilliant Career* and the *Mad Max* series. In 1976, Bruce Petty, the cartoonist, won an Oscar for the best animated film, a short humorous work entitled *Leisure*. In literature, Patrick White won the Nobel Prize in 1973, and Thomas Keneally won the 1982 Booker Prize, Britain's most prestigious literary award, for his *Schindler's Ark*, recounting the story of a German businessman who had secretly helped Jews in Nazi Germany. The poetry of Les Murray, who has written long and moving celebrations of the central coast district of New South Wales, of Peter Porter, an expatriate poet living in London, and of A. D. Hope, is studied at universities throughout Europe and the United States.

At a more popular level of the arts, Jim Sharman, the stage and film director, took *Jesus Christ Superstar* and *The Rocky Horror Show* and turned them into mammoth entertainment successes all over the world. Australian rock groups have entered the record charts in the United States and in England. Satirist Barry Humphries has had such a success with send-ups of archetypal Aussie characters—most notably Dame Edna Everage, "housewife superstar"—that he divides his time between London and Portugal, paying only fleeting visits to the country which is the source of his characters. Include the successes of the long-established greats—the Sutherlands, Helpmanns and Williamsons—and it seems that, for such a small population, Australia's achievement in the arts almost rivals its achievement in sport.

However, to judge the arts by their fame overseas is to indulge in what Australians disparagingly refer to as the "cultural cringe"—the assumption that artistic works only have merit if they have achieved success abroad. Most of the action occurs at home, and foreign audiences rarely get to hear about it. The theatre, for instance, has been through an extraordinary renaissance, but many of the plays written by local dramatists are so unabashedly Australian in their theme and language that only a handful have been performed elsewhere. Ray Lawler's *Summer of the Seventeenth Doll*, about Queensland canecutters, and Alan Seymour's *The One Day of the Year*, which explored the generation gap as exposed by Anzac Day, were the forerunners of this movement. It did not achieve its full expression, however, until the early 1970s when a radical, political, experimental drama emerged for the first time in Melbourne at two "fringe" theatres, La Mama's and the Pram Factory.

The playwrights who emerged then went on to become the nation's leading dramatists: Jack Hibberd, whose one-man play *A Stretch of the Imagination*, a virtuoso piece that takes a laconic look at the nation's bush and mateship traditions, is one of the finest pieces of theatre written in Australia; and David Williamson, who has written a series of satirical, topical plays, including *The Club*, about wheeling and dealing in the Australian Rules football world, and *Don's Party*, a play—and later made into a film—about "upwardly mobile" Labor supporters attending a raucous election-eve party.

Australian painting and sculpture have had more international success

5

than the theatre, but again the most important creative work has been done inside the country. Until his death in 1982, Fred Williams was a dominant figure, and arguably the best landscape painter in a tradition which includes such major figures as Tom Roberts, Arthur Streeton and Russell Drysdale. In the course of a lifetime's prolific work, Williams created an abstract yet still recognizable vision of the Australian bush which has become as pervasive in the iconography of the country as the earlier sunlight-and-gumtrees imagery of Hans Heysen. Williams' vision is darker and less sentimental, but equally celebratory.

In literature, three trends have become apparent. One is the appearance of a new generation of talented women, of whom Helen Garner is typical. Her novel *Monkey Grip*, later turned into a successful film, takes a close-up look at contemporary inner-city life—drugs, feminism, rock music, the attempt to pursue an alternative lifestyle in a Melbourne ghetto. Secondly, there has been a definitive move away from the highly wrought style and symbolism that is characteristic of Patrick White, who nevertheless remains the dominant figure in Australian literature. A third significant development has been the resurgence of the short story as a major form of literature, with writers such as Peter Carey, Murray Bail, Frank Moorhouse, Peter Cowan, Beverley Farmer and James McQueen revitalizing a tradition begun by Henry Lawson and the *Bulletin* school in the 1890s. Their best work tends to be laconic, experimental and urban, characterized by irony.

Classical music, opera and ballet all expanded during the 1970s, although in the 1980s there was a cutback in federal government subsidies to the performing arts. Music has always tended to be more energetic in performance than in composition, and Australia has produced several major orchestras, chamber groups and opera companies. Composers such as Richard Meale, Peter Sculthorpe, Anne Boyd, Moya Henderson, Nigel Butterley and Graham Koehne, however, have their new work performed by local groups and they are helped by occasional commissions from the Australian Broadcasting Commission, which is the main outlet for orchestral music.

The arts in Australia today are viable, visible and popular, and the cultural ferment they reflect may indeed suggest that the nation still deserves its famous sobriquet of "the lucky country". Today's Australians have inherited a continent that has the climate, the natural resources and the sort of living standards that European navigators and explorers could never have dreamt of when they set out in small, leaky sailing ships to discover the Great South Land. Not that the country is a South Pacific Utopia of the sort which Tahiti once promised to be; it is too vast, too extreme and too challenging for that. One of the nation's most popular ski resorts is a valley which early bushmen named The Perisher for its threatening and intractable climate. Its present comfortable affluence is both a result and a symbol of the brute determination of the earlier generations to make the most of what this alien, un-European and sometimes hostile continent had to offer.

Australia began its present history as one of the worst penal colonies in the world. In less than two centuries it has developed into a wealthy, suburban society characterized by some commentators as perhaps the most middle-class of all nations. Yet other voices have also been raised to point out shortcomings. Since the early 1970s, Australia, like many Western countries, has been struck by high unemployment, inflation, economic recession and damaging political crises. Some say that the old Australian traditions of egalitarianism and a fair go for all have been submerged beneath a more ruthless and competitive ethic, and that the extremes of society have drawn further apart. Certainly Australia has become more and more like other developed societies: it confronts pollution, social divisiveness, violence, exploitation, dole queues and the universal threat of nuclear war.

And yet the nation still feels optimistic. In their everyday lives, most Australians still display a lively affirmation of life. There are queues eager to buy in the supermarkets, and sun-oiled bodies strewn on the beaches. At weekends, families load up the car and head for the coast, or the outback, or a visit to the oldies, as parents are fondly known. At the end of each year, the schools pour out hundreds of thousands of turbulent, unfazed, cosmopolitan youngsters, some now with Italian profiles or Asian skins, who disappear into jobs or colleges, or overseas—although some will now end up on the dole.

At heart, they are a cheerful and pleasure-loving people, and, as the 19th-century British historian J. A. Froude described it after visiting the country, "It is hard to quarrel with men who only wish to be innocently happy." One can only wonder whether the latter years of the explosive 20th century will allow that happiness to continue undisturbed.

URBAN STREET ART

Girls playing basketball in a Sydney playground blend with a background mural.

A bush scene brightens up a garage.

A Darwin youth pauses by an Art Deco face.

In Alice Springs, women pass a supermarket mural depicting vignettes of outback life.

The desire to beautify Australia's urban sprawl has produced a crop of striking murals in towns across the nation. The boldly coloured works are usually commissioned by municipal authorities, and the artists draw their inspiration from sources as diverse as fashion magazines and surrealist art. Particularly popular are scenes of life in the outback, featuring such picturesque motifs as windmills and the camels that used to serve as draught animals in desert areas.

THE OCEAN PLAYGROUND

A warm climate and a welcoming coastline have made the sea Australia's playground. Each summer, hundreds of thousands of sun-loving hedonists head daily for the sand, which is usually within easy reach; three quarters of the population live within 80 kilometres of the shore, and Sydney alone has some 30 ocean beaches.

Aside from the universal pleasures of swimming and sunbathing, boating ranks as the most popular marine recreation. As far back as early colonial times, rowing contests were held between rival crews in ships' longboats. Leisure sailing developed in the course of the 19th century, and now squadrons of amateur sailors weigh anchor every weekend in a plethora of craft ranging from 4-metre-long skiffs to power boats and ocean-going yachts. Racing remains popular, and the international competitiveness of the nation's yachtsmen was confirmed in 1983, when an Australian vessel became the first boat in 132 years to wrest the America's Cup from its long-term holders, the New York Yacht Club.

Surfboard riding, an art originating among Pacific islanders and popularized in the United States, developed into a nationwide craze in Australia after the introduction of lightweight boards in the 1950s. Soon it had its own jargon and lifestyle, as well as heroes such as Bernard "Midget" Farrelly of New South Wales who, in 1964, became surfing's first world champion. Today about half a million Australians surf, but the sport's predominance is challenged by the growing vogue for windsurfing, an offshoot of conventional sailing that adds some of the thrills of boat-handling to the surfer's close communion with the waves.

Crew members of an American yacht participating in the 1,100-kilometre Sydney to Hobart Race sit with legs dangling over the side of their heeling vessel while spectator craft escort them out of Sydney Harbour. The race attracts some 80 yachts annually in spite of high seas and gale-force winds.

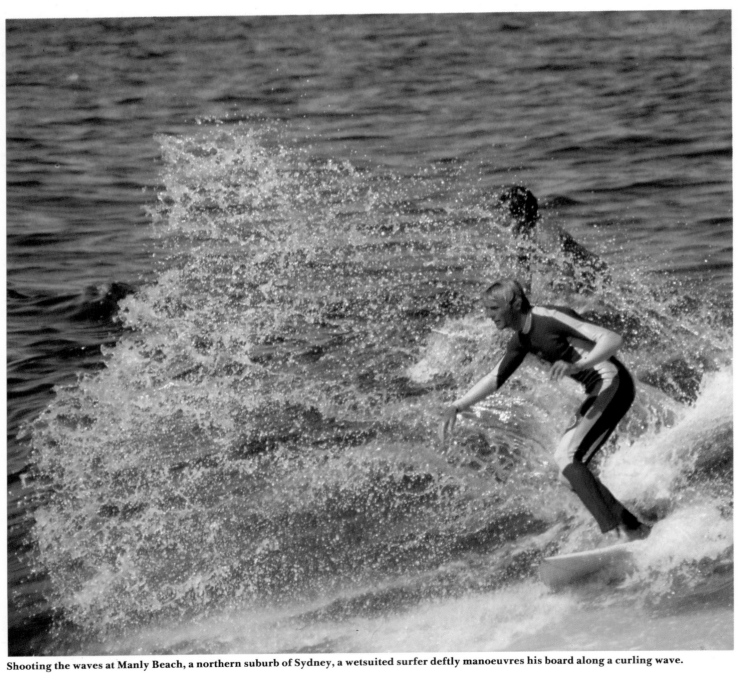

Shooting the waves at Manly Beach, a northern suburb of Sydney, a wetsuited surfer deftly manoeuvres his board along a curling wave.

Losing his balance but not his board, which is firmly attached to his ankle by a tether-rope, the same surfer wipes out a few moments later.

At the start of the windsurfing race that forms part of the annual Festival of Sydney, a small armada of entrants sets off from Manly Beach. Popular since the late 1960s, windsurfing has rapidly become a competitive sport, and fleets sometimes 200 strong enter national and world title contests.

The wooded cliffs of Barranjoey Head at the north end of Palm Beach in New South Wales loom behind a windsurfer as he controls his slight craft in a stiff Pacific breeze. To steer the 3-metre-long, 27-kilogram polyurethane board he changes the sail's position with the help of a wishbone-shaped boom.

A flotilla of pleasure-boats headed by a majestic schooner surrounds six ferry-boats competing in the annual Sydney Harbour Ferrython, a lighthearted highlight of the January-long Sydney Festival. Ferry services linking outlying districts with the city centre began in the 19th century, and despite growing competition from cars and hydrofoils they still provide commuters from some suburbs with an attractively old-fashioned way of crossing the congested metropolis.

ACKNOWLEDGEMENTS

The index for this book was prepared by Vicki Robinson. For their help in the preparation of this volume, the editors wish to thank: Agent General for South Australia, London; Agent General for Victoria, London; Library, Australian High Commission, London; Australian Tourist Commission, London; Francesca Baas-Becking, Australian Institute of Aboriginal Studies, Canberra; Baiba Berzins, Mitchell Library, State Library of New South Wales, Sydney; Broken Hill Proprietary Co. Ltd., London; John W. Brown, Government of Western Australia, London; Chartair, Alice Springs; Flinders Bookshop, London; Freshwater Surf Life Saving Club, Sydney; Noel Fullerton, Virginia Camel Safaris, Alice Springs; Alistair J. Gilmour, Great Barrier Reef Marine Park Authority, Townsville, Queensland; Anne-Louise Graham Bell, Sydney; Fred Hockley, Director, School of the Air, Alice Springs; Elizabeth Hodgson, London; Keith Hope, Department of State Development, South Australian Government, Adelaide; H.L. Keelan, Broken Hill Library, City of Broken Hill, New South Wales; Stephen Langhorn, Agent General for New South Wales, London; Jimmy Lucas, Department of Photographs, Imperial War Museum, London; Heinz Luik, Alice Springs Federal Casino, Alice Springs; Brian Males, Royal Flying Doctor Service, Alice Springs; Librarian, Botany Department, Natural History Museum, London; North Crenella Surf Life Saving Club, Sydney; North Narabeen Surf Life Saving Club, Sydney; Reg O'Grady, Agent General for Queensland, London; Mike O'Hanlan, Museum of Mankind, London; Queenscliffe Surf Life Saving Club, Sydney; K.A. Richards, North Broken Hill Holdings Ltd., Melbourne; Malcolm Roberts, Cattlemen's Association, Alice Springs; Frank Strahan, The University of Melbourne Archives, Carlton, Victoria; Bill and June Tapp, Killarney Station, Northern Territory; Public Relations Director, University of Sydney; Bob Watt, "The Centralian", Alice Springs.

BIBLIOGRAPHY

BOOKS

Aitken, Jonathan, *Land of Fortune*. Martin Secker & Warburg, London, 1971.

Allen, Oliver E., and the Editors of Time-Life Books, *The Pacific Navigators*. Time-Life Books, Amsterdam, 1980.

Australian Mineral Industry Annual Review for 1981. Australian Government Publishing Service, 1984.

Baglin, Douglass, and Mullins, Barbara, *The Book of Australia*. Summit Books, Sydney, 1973.

Berndt, Ronald M., ed., *Australian Aboriginal Art*. Collier–Macmillan, Middlesex, 1964.

Blainey, Geoffrey, *The Rise of Broken Hill*. Macmillan, London, 1968.

Blainey, Geoffrey, *Triumph of the Nomads*. The Macmillan Press, London, 1976.

Boehm, A. E., *Twentieth Century Economic Development in Australia*. Longman Cheshire, Melbourne, 1971.

Broom, Leonard, and Lancaster Jones, F., *A Blanket a Year*. Australian National University Press, 1973.

Burton, Barbara, and Splatt, William, *100 Masterpieces of Australian Painting*. John Currey O'Neil Publishers, Australia, 1981.

Cameron, R. J., *Year Book Australia*. Australian Bureau of Statistics, 1983.

Carroll, John B., ed., *Intruders in the Bush*. Oxford University Press, 1982.

Chisholm, A. H., and Serventy, Vincent, *John Gould's The Birds of Australia*. Lansdowne Press, Sydney, 1973.

Cobbe, Hugh, ed., *Cook's Voyages and Peoples of the Pacific*. British Museum Publications, 1979.

Coghill, I., *Australia's Mineral Resources*. Sorrett Publishers, 1971.

Cornelia, Elizabeth, *Australia: The Land and Its People*. Macdonald Educational, London, 1977.

Crowley, Frank, ed., *A New History of Australia*. Heinemann, Melbourne, 1974.

Davies, David M., *The Last of the Tasmanians*. Frederick Muller, London, 1973.

Flood, Josephine, *Archaeology of the Dreamtime*. William Collins, Sydney, 1983.

Fodor's Australia, New Zealand and the South Pacific. Hodder & Stoughton, London, 1984.

Fraser, Bryce, *The Macquarie Book of Australian Events*. The Macquarie Library, 1983.

Fuente, Dr. Felix Rodriguez de la, *Animals of Australasia*. Orbis, London, 1971.

Griffin, J., ed., *Essays in the Economic History of Australia*. Jacaranda Press, 1967.

History of Commerce and Industry in Western Australia,
A. University of Western Australia Press, 1981.

Horne, Donald, *The Lucky Country*. Penguin Books London, 1964.

Howard, Colin, *Australia's Constitution*. Penguin Books Australia, 1978.

Hughes, Robert, *The Art of Australia*. Penguin Books, London, 1970.

Idriess, Ion L., *Lasseter's Last Ride*. Jonathan Cape, London, 1936.

Kearns, R. H. B., *Broken Hill: A Pictorial History*. Investigator Press, Australia, 1982.

Keneally, Thomas, *Outback*. Hodder & Stoughton, London, 1983.

Kynaston, Edward, *The Penguin Book of the Bush*. Penguin Books, London, 1977.

Lacour-Gayet, Robert, *A Concise History of Australia*. Penguin Books, London, 1976.

Laffin, John, *Anzacs at War*. Abelard–Schuman, London, 1965.

Marshall, Catherine, *Thorn Bird Country*. Thames & Hudson, London, 1983.

McGregor, Craig, *The Australian People*. Hodder & Stoughton, New South Wales, 1980.

McGregor, Craig, and the Editors of Time-Life Books, *The Great Barrier Reef*. Time-Life Books, Amsterdam, 1974.

McGregor, Craig, *Profile of Australia*. Penguin Books, London, 1968.

McLeod, A. L., ed., *The Pattern of Australian Culture*. Cornell University Press, New York, 1963.

McLuckie, John, and McKee, H. S., *Australian and New Zealand Botany*. Horwitz Publications Inc., Sydney, 1954.

Minerals and Mineral Development. Department of Resources Development Western Australia, 1984.

Moffitt, Ian, and the Editors of Time-Life Books, *The Australian Outback*. Time-Life Books, 1976.

Morcombe, Michael, *An Illustrated Encyclopaedia of Australian Wildlife*. The Macmillan Company of Australia, Melbourne, 1974.

Nomination of the Great Barrier Reef for Inclusion in the World Heritage List. Great Barrier Reef Marine Park Authority, 1981.

Norton, W. R., *The Deterioration in Economic Performance*. Reserve Bank of Australia.

OECD Economic Surveys 1982–1983, Australia. OECD, 1983.

Paynting, H. H., ed., *The James Flood Book of Early Australian Photographs*. The James Flood Charity Trust, 1970.

Peach's Australian Cities. Australian Broadcasting Commission, 1980.

Pearling in Western Australia. Department of Fisheries & Wildlife, 1981.

Porter, Peter, and the Editors of Time-Life Books, *Sydney*. Time-Life Books, Amsterdam, 1980.

Queensland Resources Atlas. State Public Relations Bureau, Brisbane, 1980.

Rienits, Rex and Thea, *A Pictorial History of Australia*. Paul Hamlyn, Sydney, 1978.

Rienits, Rex and Thea, *The Voyages of Captain Cook*. The Hamlyn Publishing Group, Middlesex, 1968.

Shaw, A. G. L., *The Story of Australia*. Faber & Faber, London, 1983.

Slater, Peter, *A Field Guide to Australian Birds*. Scottish Academic Press, Edinburgh, 1970.

Smith, Bernard, *Australian Painting 1788–1970*. Oxford University Press, 1971.

The South West Book, A Tasmanian Wilderness. Australian Conservation Commission, 1978.

Spearritt, Peter, and Walker, David, eds., *Australian Popular Culture*. George Allen & Unwin, Australia, 1979.

Stokes, Edward, *United We Stand*. The Five Mile Press, Australia, 1983.

Stone, C. R., *Australian Landforms*. Wren Publishing, Australia, 1974.

Suter, Keith D., and Stearman, Kaye, *Aboriginal Australians*. Minority Rights Group, 1982.

Sykes, T., *The Money Miners*. Wildcat Press, 1978.

Thiele, Colin, *The Adelaide Story*. Television Broadcasters Ltd., 1982.

This is Australia. Lansdowne Press, Sydney, 1982.

Thomas, Laurie, ed., *200 Years of Australian Painting*. Bay Books, Australia, 1971.

Tullock, John, *Australian Cinema*. George Allen & Unwin, Australia, 1982.

Ward, Russel, *The Australian Legend*. Oxford University Press, 1958.

Whitaker, Donald P., *Area Handbook for Australia*. The American University, 1974.

Wright, Judith, *The Cry for the Dead*. OUP, 1981.

Yeomans, John, *The Scarce Australians*. Longmans, Green & Co. Ltd., London, 1967.

PERIODICALS

Abercrombe, Thomas, J., "Perth—Fair Winds and Full Sails." *National Geographic*, May 1982.

British Empire series, Time-Life Books:
  "The World Revealed." No. 11,
  "Early Days Down Under." No. 13,
  "Australia Strikes It Rich." No. 42,
  "Opening the Outback." No. 43.

Brennan, Niall, "The Last of the Camel Men." *GEO*, Australia, June–August 1982.

Burger, Angela, "Brisbane—A Little Bit Country." *GEO*, Australia, September–November, 1982.

Canby, Thomas Y., "El Niño's Ill Wind." *National Geographic*, February 1984.

Caras, Roger, "What's a Koala?." *GEO*, U.S.A.,

May 1983.

Duncan Tim, "The Garden State Runs Dry." *The Bulletin*, January 18, 1983.

Financial Times Survey—Australia, *Financial Times*, November 8, 1982.

Garwood, Roger, "Twenty Fathoms Under the Sea." *Western Australia*, Spring 1981.

Grenard, Philip, "Schools With a Dash of Color." *The Bulletin*, August 17, 1982.

Grenard, Philip, and Speirs, Neil, "The New Asian Invasion." *The Bulletin*, August 16, 1983.

Guppy, Daryl, "White Cliffs, Dark Opals." *GEO, Australia*, March–May 1983.

Holmes, Rosemary, "White Man's Hole in the Ground." *GEO, Australia*, March–May 1983.

Hoyle, Russ, "Australia's 'Great Dry'." *Time*, March 28, 1983.

"In the Deep End—Bob Hawke's Australia: A Survey." *The Economist*, August 6, 1983.

Knightley, Phillip, "Once and Future Kings." *Sunday Times Magazine*, October 2, 1983.

Knightley, Phillip, "Skirmish in Paradise." *Sunday Times Magazine*, July 10, 1983.

McIlwraith, John, "Salt—The White Harvest." *Western Australia*, Autumn 1982.

Moore, Kenny, "Coober Pedy—Opal Capital of Australia's Outback." *National Geographic*, October 1976.

Nicklin, Lenore, "The Wednesday Two States Burned to Ashes." *The Bulletin*, March 1, 1983.

"Save the Kangaroo." *The Listener*, March 8, 1984.

Schraps, Wolfgang, "Der Energie–Sparer." *GEO*, Germany, November 1982.

Scollay, Clive, "Arnhem Land Aboriginals Cling to Dreamtime." *National Geographic*, November 1980.

Segal, David, "Angels of the Outback." *GEO, Australia*, March–May 1982.

Souter, Gavin, "Bizarre Folk Hero." *Smithsonian*, June 1983.

Stevens, Joan, "Tasmania's South–West." *GEO, Australia*, 1980.

Stokes, Edward, "Broken Hill: Where Has All the Silver Gone." *GEO, Australia*, 1979.

Templin, Jenny, "Lifesavers." *Journey*, December 1982–February 1983.

Times Special Report, *The Times*, October 12, 1983.

Times Special Report, *The Times*, September 15, 1982.

Tropical Cyclone Warning Centre, staff of, "Looking a Storm in the Eye." *GEO, Australia*, 1979.

White, Paul William, "At Grips With An Island State of Mind." *The Bulletin*, November 16, 1982.

Wilesmith, Greg, "Land Rights Become Reality." *The Bulletin*, May 10, 1983.

INDEX

Page numbers in italics refer to illustrations or to illustrated text.

Colour separations by City Ensign Group,
Hull, England.
Phototypesetting by Tradespools Ltd.,
Frome, Somerset.
Printed and bound by Artes Gráficas
Toledo, S.A., Spain.
D.L.TO:42-1990